TODAY'S INSPIRED LATINA™

Volume IX

LIFE STORIES OF SUCCESS IN THE FACE OF ADVERSITY

JACQUELINE S. RUIZ

Today's Inspired Latina

This book is a compilation of stories from numerous people who have each contributed a chapter and is designed to provide inspiration to our readers.

It is sold with the understanding that the publisher and the individual authors are not engaged in the rendering of psychological, legal, accounting or other professional advice. The content and views in each chapter are the sole expression and opinion of its author and not necessarily the views of Fig Factor Media, LLC.

For more information, contact:

Fig Factor Media, LLC | www.figfactormedia.com
Today's Inspired Latina | www.todayslatina.com

Cover Design & Layout by Juan Pablo Ruiz
Printed in the United States of America

ISBN: 978-1-952779-99-2

I dedicate this amazing book to the global community that we have built together. This community has allowed the *Today's Inspired Latina* series to flourish and become a success. An achievement that proves there is a demand and magic to be found in the pages of what we have worked so hard to create.

Table of Contents:

Acknowledgements

I would first like to take the time to thank all of the incredible team members who made *Today's Inspired Latina Volume IX*, a reality. Thank you, Gaby Hernández Franch, for being the wings of Fig Factor Media and continuing to expand our reach.

Thank you, Irene Balado for coming back as the project manager for *Today's Inspired Latina Volume IX*, as well as our editors in your team. Thank you both for the countless hours, all the follow-ups, all the love, all the words, all the creativity, and everything you have put into this volume. But thank you most of all for elevating the stories of these 20 incredible authors.

I would like to thank our designer Manuel Serna for continuing to extend the *Today's Inspired Latina* brand beyond just a book with different modalities of the brand—all with the purpose of elevating women around the world.

I would also like to extend thanks to my husband, Juan Pablo Ruiz, without whom this project would not have been possible. Thank you for helping me create the *Today's Inspired Latina* brand that has now become global. *Today's Inspired Latina* has been registered in the United States, Mexico, and Central Europe, and I owe this success to your help and unwavering support.

And of course, I want to thank all the women that came before Volume IX because they have believed in me throughout the launch and success of this brand—especially the women from Volume I. When we first launched *Today's Inspired Latina*, we didn't even include a volume number because it was supposed to be one book with ten women. Those ten women turned into 27, and one book turned into many other volumes. Now we are sharing Volume IX with the world. We continue to share the magic, inspiration, and love for the stories, authors, and everything we're doing.

- JACQUELINE S. RUIZ

Introduction

Welcoming a new book into the world is never not cause for celebration, but when releasing the ninth edition of a book that has touched the lives of thousands around the world comes to fruition, you celebrate all that has come before. To publish nine of anything is to bear witness to magic—the magic of success and the chance to share stories from women of all backgrounds. To be able to continue to share the success stories of our authors and the trials along the way has been a privilege that has humbled me in many ways. Today's Inspired Latina authors have come together to help us shine a light on the beauty created when we become cognoscente of the impact that we make together.

When I first dreamed up the Today's Inspired Latina book, it was just that, a single, standalone book. With only ten other authors, we could not have imagined how far the dream would continue. Those ten authors soon turned into 23. And that one single book turned into Volume IX. I am so humbled to share these Latina's stories with you, and I am incredibly excited to continue to look to the future for the Today's Inspired Latina series. In volume IX, you will witness the strength and courage all these Latinas have in common. Our authors have continued to inspire me throughout this beautiful journey. Every woman who has been a part of the last nine volumes has helped us create magic—all 218 authors. So, while we look to the present to celebrate our victories, it is also because of these 218 authors that we can widen our reach. We have created magic, and we will continue to create magic as long as there remain Latina women willing to share their stories with us. The success of the series has been incredible and would not be possible without the help of these authors and our readers. So, we share today in hopes that we will inspire a brighter future for Latina women everywhere around the world.

Today's Inspired Latina has become a way for us to share with the world the power and strength of Latinas worldwide. What started as a passion project has become so much more. Creating the Today's Inspired Latina book has led to an expansion of products and series and lectures that would not have been possible without the first edition authors. It is with their inspiration that the series has indeed spread its wings and taken flight. Born from the inspiration of TIL, LatinaTalks has allowed our authors to communicate in real-time their experiences through speaking engagements. We have also been fortunate enough to reach Latinas of all ages by creating the Today's Inspire Young Latina series. With three published volumes, young Latina's worldwide have also been able to participate in Young LatinaTalks, which have recorded 60 plus talks around the United States. We have even been able to create the Today's Inspired Latina "Stories of Impact Around the World" Board Game to continue to share the perseverance these women all inspire.

There is so much magic to be shared. In a world where representation isn't always a given, the Today's Inspired Latina series aims to help fight a lack of representation and help share the stories of the most inspirational Latinas of our time. Today's Inspired Latina is currently available in 25 countries, and we are continuing to expand our wings every day. I am so excited to see what this journey has in store for all of these incredible authors. I have watched in awe as they have found their footing and started to grow within themselves. They have already done the hard work of learning how to share all that makes them unique with the world. Now they continue to grow as they allow their work to be released into the world. They are an inspiration because of the incredible magic they all spread.

Over the last nine volumes, there have been times where I have been humbled and times when I have been so incredibly excited for all our authors. Today, many of the women we have had the opportunity to work with have created their own personal brands. They had the opportunity to learn through the authorship process that their stories deserve to be heard and that there is a demand to learn from their experiences. It has been so inspiring to watch as these authors have taken the Today's Inspired Latina authorship as an opportunity to spread their wings to further their professional aspirations. I have watched as they have discovered themselves, and I've bear witness to many of these authors finding a way to share what they believe with the world. Whether through branding, books, products, or public speaking opportunities. These Latinas never cease to amaze me. Authorship is certainly not the limit for these women. They have created movements, nonprofit organizations, their own brand, and they have become members of important boards. They've traveled the world, they've connected with each other, and are continuing to create. Embarking on this journey with these incredible women has been such a privilege. They have shared their stories with me and shown me the true meaning of perseverance by spreading the magic of the project around the globe.

It has been an absolutely amazing journey for me to bear witness to. So, with Volume IX, I want to take the time to not only congratulate these women on sharing their truth with the world, but I want to celebrate the many organizations and opportunities created by my fellow book sisters, as we all call each other. You have done it. You have shared your story and, in the process, created absolute magic beyond it.

- JACQUELINE S. RUIZ

Preface

BY SANJIV CHOPRA

Steve Jobs once said, "The most powerful people in the world are story tellers."

In this issue of Todays Inspired Latina you will read some amazing stories of resilience, perseverance, passion, and overcoming many an adversity and finding fulfillment in life by virtue of finding one's purpose and living it.

I have had the privilege of now knowing Jackie Camacho for about two years.

I was honored when she invited me to give a Keynote to Two-Hundred Latina Inspired Women in Puerto Vallarta, Mexico in 2019.

It was a gratifying moment because I met so many luminous and inspiring leaders. Each one's story was moving yet uplifting. Everyone in the room was happy when they first walked in, and even happier at the end of the event.

Allow me to share with you a few reflections on happiness. Albert Schweitzer, physician, theologian, humanitarian and Nobel Laureate once said, "Success is not the key to happiness. Happiness is the key to success."

The happiest people on this planet have four things in common.

1. A cadre of good friends
2. The ability to forgive
3. Serving others
4. Expressing gratitude

However, happiness is more than the sum total of happy moments. In order for us to have sustained happiness we have to find our purpose and live it. Mark Twain once famously said "The two most important days in your life are the day you are born and the day you find out why".

Many of the story tellers in this volume of Todays Inspired Latina have displayed enormous courage, fortitude and grit and found their purpose in life. They are inspiring legions of others in their footsteps and we collectively owe them a great debt of gratitude.

Kudos to Jackie Camacho-Ruiz for her continued, creative, and impactful leadership.

Sanjiv Chopra, M.B.B.S., M.A.C.P. FRCP (London)
Professor of Medicine
Harvard Medical School
Best-Selling Author
Sought after speaker
sanjivchopra.com

Maggie Antillon-Mathews

*"Always be there for others. Always inspire them with your
dreams and hope, vision and mission, attitude and aptitude."*

Once again, I am presented with the opportunity to share
my story in another collaboration book filled with narratives like
mine. Four years have passed since I told my story of being a first-
generation American, born to Mexican parents, who emigrated
from Northern Mexico searching for the American dream. I
shared with you the lessons my parents taught me about hard
work and dedication and the importance of always giving back.
I also shared my journey- one that catapulted me from a career
in social work to a prosperous career in real estate. I recounted
my most terrifying and darkest moments, like not being able to
afford a $25 baggage fee during a trip, let alone my mortgage and
utilities. Most importantly, I shared the story of how I overcame
all the obstacles despite my struggles with depression and anxiety;
reliving all my most vulnerable and painful insecurities and
downfalls, yet despite it all, I always found a way to keep moving
forward and prosper.

A lot has changed in the last four years, yet not with a whole
new set of obstacles, forks in the road, and continued lessons and
teachings.

IN THE WAKE OF UNCERTAINTY IS WHEN YOU TRULY DISCOVER THAT "LIFE IS WHAT HAPPENS WHEN YOU ARE BUSY MAKING OTHER PLANS"

2020 was a year that, for all of us, changed everything. For me, it changed my perspective. Everything that I thought about, the plans I thought I wanted to make, how I went about my daily routine, ran my business, family life, social interactions with friends, colleagues, and clients all changed. The world suddenly stopped, and things, as we knew them, would never be the same. The government issued a stay-at-home order, and schools, restaurants, and businesses were forced to close. There was so much uncertainty, and no one knew exactly how this would all play out. The global pandemic sat us all down and forced us to stop, look and listen. It forced us to reflect on our everyday routines.

Accustomed to my fast-paced life as a businesswoman, it was the first time in my career that I was not expected to do what I thought defined me. I quickly realized that for many years I had given the best of myself to my business, my clients, and my agents, while giving the rest of myself to my family. I lost 40 lbs. in two years and had no energy. I could not eat anything, and I could barely put mac and cheese in the microwave for my daughter. Somehow, in the face of uncertainty, I knew I was in the exact place I needed to be, at the precise time I needed to be there.

FOR I KNOW THE PLANS I HAVE FOR YOU

What I have learned through my faith in God is that this too, would be a time for change and growth. He knows the plans, and He is the only one who will decide the way; He already has.

Just as I had to turn my failed business around in 2008 when the real estate market crashed and burned to the ground, I knew I would be able to learn the lessons and rise again. Yet, this time was different, this time I was ready. I planned to weather the storm, I planned to use the knowledge I acquired during those tumultuous years to continue my intended journey. In 2008 I managed to survive. In 2020 there was no doubt in my mind that I would survive and thrive.

Who could have predicted the current state of the market? The pandemic led to a surge in demand, causing homes to sell quickly in competitive market conditions, which meant I was busy, busier than I had ever been. I had the honor of being featured in Chicago Agent Magazine. Also, the Chicago Association of Realtors awarded me the Top Producer Award and the NATIONAL ASSOCIATION OF HISPANIC REAL ESTATE PROFESSIONALS (NAHREP) named me in the top 250 agents. Finally, I was awarded top producer within my real estate company. Not only did I weather the storm, but I also rode the wave and went on to have the most successful year in my career.

THE REAL HEROES AND THE SUPERSTARS

"I think a hero is any person really intent on making this a better place for all people." – Maya Angelou

I have always wanted to make this world a better place, to be the change I wanted to see, and inspire others. Throughout this journey, many powerful women I admire and have followed throughout the years, have inspired me to keep going, and be a leader and an agent of change. Local leaders and mentors such as Marki Lemons-Ryhal and Baxtie Rodriguez, both trailblazers in my industry, have helped pave the road.

I have learned there are no limits to what women can accomplish. Our work has not gone unnoticed, and today, the conversations are different. Women are in leadership roles and are sitting at the table making decisions.

Excelling in my career means that other realtors walking through the doors of my brokerage, looking for someone who cares and can help them achieve their goals, will find them. It is about inspiring that one person in the room who believes they cannot do it and encouraging them to think they can. It is about helping them silence that negative voice of self-doubt and helping them understand sometimes it takes others to believe in you more than you believe in yourself. That has been the case for me many times. Being a mentor to others strengthens the belief that my purpose has always been to help people. While I have the opportunity to mentor them, in reality, it is they who inspire me.

THE PURPOSE OF LIFE IS A LIFE OF PURPOSE

The women I mentor have full-time jobs, thriving careers, children, and a household, yet they seem to do it all with heart and grace. While helping, inspiring, and mentoring others brings me joy, there are days when I am the one who needs to be encouraged. I draw upon these mentors and superheroes. I consider myself a product of a series of failures, but I learned true success lies in doing it all and still being successful. I will continue to mentor and inspire women, and I am focused on the future woman my daughter will become. I am constantly evolving and growing both professionally and personally. However, certain aspects of my life are still a work in progress. There is no growth if we do not continue to work on ourselves, constantly reinvent ourselves, and ask "what's next?"

WHEN FACED WITH ADVERSITY, HOW DO I INSPIRE OTHERS TO ACHIEVE SUCCESS?

"Success is the culmination of failures, mistakes, false starts, confusion, and the determination to keep going." – Nick Gleason

To those looking to achieve success, I say, find your passion. Find what moves you, what drives you, and what excites you, then do that. I owe my success to all of my many, many failures. I am armed with knowledge because, throughout my career and my life, I tried and failed and tried again. The secret to my success is simple- Do. Not. Give. Up! That is the same advice I will continue to give my daughter and the future generation of young women who will become the leaders of tomorrow. Make mistakes, learn from them and grow. When you set a goal, there are the inevitable lows. You face rejection, and there are plenty of distractions and negativity. Learn to focus on the positive and ignore the negative.

Trying to achieve your goals can sometimes feel like you are trying to get ahead while running through an obstacle course that only goes in circles. It may seem as if those who came before you had a clear, straight path to success, and your road is rocky and full of bumps- the one less traveled- and perhaps that may be true, but I learned the finish line is the same whether we take the narrow winding road or the short, unpaved road. We get to where we are meant to be.

SUCCESS IS MEASURED IN YEARS

As I come close to celebrating my twentieth anniversary as a Realtor, I am reminded of a quote by singer and comedian Eddie Cantor, who said, *"It takes twenty years to be an overnight success."* While some may see me as a success story and measure my success by my accomplishments, the truth is that being successful has always been an uphill battle and roller coaster for me. Behind the smile in the pictures or social media posts lies a story of plenty of fear, tears, and sacrifices. My road has been rocky and filled with many twists and turns and that still stands today. I believe that the secret to my success has always been consistency with my intentions of always working in good faith.

Although I am proud of what I have accomplished, the occasional negative voice of self-doubt likes to creep up on me. While I still need to work on the feelings of self-doubt and worry, today, the conversation I have with myself is different.

I focus on growing through every experience to help me achieve my goals. Going into this next phase of my professional and personal life, it is no longer about how something or someone can make me happy and fulfilled, but how I can do that for myself, and my mind, body, soul, and life.

I am continuously trying to better myself and all the aspects of my life, but more than ever, my home and my family, along with my health, and peace are my priority. I learned many things in life, but mainly that every path and road we take are either rewards or lessons you take onto the next step and direction. I know the light guide for me has been God, and through his grace and mercy, I am still here.

I firmly believe everything happens for a reason, and there is always a lesson. When you look back at any negative experience in your life, you see how it has molded you to be the person you are today, and you are stronger because of it; this time has not only taught us to be strong, but also to be vulnerable.

Thankfully, I do not have to endure this incredible undertaking alone. I am blessed and beyond thankful to be surrounded by my family. My husband, parents, and family make it possible for me to succeed and follow my passion with purpose. Without them, my success is not possible.

I was not supposed to write this story. I called the publisher twice and told her I was not in the right place; my life was not perfect, and I was a work in progress. Her response? "Perfect, we all are." However, I am inspired by all the strong women who have believed in me, the ones who have helped me find my purpose, my heroes that give me the energy to keep going. Going through the process of writing this story has proven to be therapeutic. Telling my story has allowed me to go through this process of growth, clarity, and self-awareness. I recommend that we all take the time to tell our story, as we are all authors of our own best-selling book.

I look forward to the next chapter that God has already planned out for me and thankful every day for the opportunity to keep growing.

REFLECTION QUESTIONS

1. What battles have you overcome in your life and what did you learn from it?

2. What do you define as success?

3. What would you like your legacy to be?

BIOGRAPHY

Maggie Antillon has been in real estate since 2001 and is currently a designated managing broker, trainer and mentor at Realty of Chicago where she has been for 6 years, after previously owning her own top producing company.

The multimillion-dollar producer, managing broker, and top agent from Chicago brings a wealth of knowledge and talent to the Chicago real estate market and has received various Top Producer awards from The Chicago Association of Realtors. She is consistently named in the TOP 250 in the nation by The National Association of Hispanic Real Estate Professionals (NAHREP) as well as a top producer at Realty of Chicago.

Maggie has also been featured repeatedly in the "Who's Who" Edition of Chicago Agent Magazine and other local publications, and she co-authored the book "Latina Empowerment Through Leadership," which was published in 2017 and quickly became a bestseller in Amazon's women's category.

She is most proud of the growth of her company and the agents she mentors. Maggie has helped take Realty of Chicago from a small real estate company to being named one of the fastest growing companies in Chicago, and #1 in the Latino market.

Maggie serves on several community boards and organizations and is constantly involved with outreach and community work, partnering with people that are consistent with her values. Today she is committed to sharing her knowledge and experiences with others looking to grow in Real Estate and an advocate for women and young ladies, including her daughter and niece by inspiring them to follow their dreams.

Maggie Antillon-Mathews
7738964922 direct
7739881688 office
www.maggiesellschicago.com

Nuvia Yesenia

"Everything in life has a beginning, but it never has an ending. Life only has miraculous transformations."

There comes a time in life when nothing makes sense anymore. The things you say and the things you do no longer align with what you want for yourself. You begin to question everything and everyone around you. You even begin to question your own existence. After I hit rock bottom, I began to have all these thoughts. I realized my whole life up to that point had been a big fat lie. The things I believed in were absurd. I took for granted every negative word anyone said about me. For some reason, I also believed that there was a tall, bearded man sitting on a throne writing out the plot of my life. I was certain enough he had defined my destiny by stating "Nuvia will trip and fall and have her heart break into pieces several times." I have always felt like a victim who is not able to stand up for herself and leaves another one to control her fate.

Life put me through many challenges and hardships, but nothing has been as hard as forgiving those who had hurt me. I worked it out. If I wanted to make the best out of my life, I would need to let go of the things that were pulling me down. I had to let go of my past though I was convinced that my happiness depended on holding to it with a tight grip. The moment I decided to release all that useless baggage from the past, everything changed for the better. Everything in life has a beginning, but it never has an ending. Life only has miraculous transformations. Nonetheless, before my transformation, I walked through the fire. Such experience only made me stronger, wiser, and a humble-hearted woman.

A DYSFUNCTIONAL CHILDHOOD

I had a very tough childhood. I dare say I had no childhood at all.

At age two, I faced the painful truth that my father did not love me. When my parents divorced, he vanished from my life, and my mother and I fell into poverty and humiliation. After some time, my mother got married again and her new husband substituted my biological father. I had to adjust to this change without complaints; I could not even pronounce the name of my dad. My "new father" was now my mother's husband. I thought it would get easier with time, but it actually got harder. When I was five, I was sexually molested by a person who used to babysit me when my mother went out with her new family. I chose to keep the secret for months, but when I finally decided to disclose it, no one believed me. Once he stopped abusing me, I had to manage to forget this horrible experience, but the nightmares would allow me no peace. Moreover, I started to feel home as hell. My mother provided my siblings and I with all of the material things we needed, but she would never give us love. I felt I was not cared for. Rather, I would feel more like a punching bag in a boxing ring— where the boxing ring was my own house. I was bullied in the place that was supposed to be safe. My mother would call me: fat, dumb, unworthy, clumsy, ungrateful, and so many other nasty words. I was beaten and belittled constantly, which in the long run revealed the worst of me. I thought I was a bad child because I could never meet her expectations.

I ran away from home when every time I could not take it anymore only to be brought back involuntarily because I was a minor. Then, I got kicked out of the house many times because I began to speak up and defend myself. I joined a band—playing the drums—and I would get kicked out of the house because of that too. Since I had neither their support nor their understanding, little by little, I gave up on my dreams. I temporarily lived in more than eleven homes before I even reached eighteen. As a consequence of such high instability, I developed an insecure personality. I was traumatized and began to isolate myself because I suffered from social phobia. Furthermore, I started having eating disorders, such as anorexia and bulimia. I usually felt depressed and attempted suicide many times. I stopped believing in myself. I gave up to the fact I would never make anything out of myself.

THE NEVER-ENDING SEARCH

This part of my life I refer to as "toxicity," because it is when I was most involved with toxic relationships and substances. I was desperately looking for my father in every partner. His absence in my life created a profound feeling of emptiness in my heart. The lack of affection from my mother made me think I was defective and not worthy of love. I was merely seeking love from scarcity, so I only attracted dysfunctional relationships. I was vulnerable and naïve, and eager for love and affection. The last time my mother threw me out of the house, I decided to marry in hopes of having a stable home. Nevertheless, I just got exactly the opposite. I happened to get married to someone who was a bad person. I was co-dependent and relied on anyone that would offer me two cents of love. I pinned my hopes on him emotionally. I finally separated after four years when I noticed I was losing myself in his shadows. I thought I would be able to make it without him; however, the lack of support pushed me to become an alcoholic.

I was still struggling with the suicidal thoughts and depression, and when alcohol was not enough to hush those voices, I found the answer in drugs. I got into drugs trying to find some peace of mind. I did it! But only the lapse of time the effect lasted. I was no longer with my toxic husband, but I kept attracting more evil people into my life. Again, I was only treated like trash; then I reaffirmed I would never be able to get away from that negative-pattern jail. I was somehow addicted to all that toxicity. I was raised neglected and I could not realize I was falling into the same trap again and again. I did not give up on love and happiness but kept going in circles. I was alone, scared, and barely surviving.

CLIMBING OUT OF THE HOLE

On April 2017, my body collapsed and got very ill. It was no surprise that after all the things I had gone through plus all I had abused of my body, I would get sick. The sensation was that of a rock beating my head. Then, it was like falling into the bottom of a deep dark hole. That was a wake-up call. I was in and out of hospitals unable to get a diagnose about what was wrong with me. I began to regret all the times I mistreated my body, but I mostly regretted not having cherished my heart. I was wrecked but desperate to find an answer. Upon the lack of solutions on the part of doctors, I began to explore on ways to heal myself. I read all sorts of books on how to achieve a good health until I discovered the vegan lifestyle. Right away, I shifted my eating habits and stopped consuming toxic substances. I started to feel better: a miracle. On top of all, this change helped me pierce the veil and begin the journey onto the path of healing my life.

After some time on my new diet, I went to see another doctor who, after all, was able to tell me why I had been sick a few months before. He diagnosed me with an autoimmune disease called polycystic ovarian syndrome or PCOS. PCOS is a hormonal disorder common among women of reproductive age. PCOS has many unpleasant and painful symptoms such as infertility, inflammation, weight gain, hair loss, problematic skin, depression, insulin resistance, mood swings, among others. Doctors do not know the cause or the why, simply that certain habits trigger symptoms—none of them in some women, many or all of them in others. I had them all. And my toxic addictions made my body scream for help! I felt weak in my knees when I began to learn more about PCOS because I knew no one who could possibly help me get better. All the doctors I visited affirmed that this disorder had no cure and that I would need medicine for the rest of my life. I simply refused to believe that my life would depend on medicine and PCOS. I decided it was my life, my health, and my destiny. So, I had what it took to heal. I dove more deeply into this vegan lifestyle and reached out for help. I hired a plant-based nutritionist who was familiar with my condition and I regained hope. Everything began to fall into place, so I decided to seek the help of a therapist. I was aware that if I wanted to heal, I had to start from the root of it all: my thoughts. I started to follow the guidelines given by the nutritionist and therapist, and I began to feel happier and healthier. Once you begin to heal one part of your life, the rest will tag along. I always tell people who know me that I was saved by the hormone because it was not till then I could begin to visualize a brighter future for me and those around me. Having PCOS has been my major blessing because I was moved to seek for better opportunities. This meant that I chose to get rid of relationships that were neither motivating nor supporting me. I had to start living a quality life full of gratitude and compassion. PCOS encouraged me to immerse into my inner self and I discovered there was an amazing being who was hiding underneath all that hate I had built over years and years towards everyone. Thanks to PCOS I was able to climb out of the hole.

OVER THE MOUNTAINS

The person I had dreamed of becoming was waiting for me over the mountains. All I had to do was to climb higher to the top to see my best version. I merged with the universe and began to set goals. Now, I do not care about all the stones I encountered on the journey, because I finally accomplished my heart's desires. A huge lesson I have learned: it is never too late to start living the life of your dreams. All those wrong turns led me to the right path. Regarding those who hurt me, I was able to forgive them all. I let go of my past and now only focus on the future I want to create for myself. All of the bad things that happened to me were only good things in disguise. Today, I share my story to inspire others. Today, I share my music with others to bring joy to their heart. I am no longer surviving because now I am LIVING.

REFLECTION QUESTIONS

1. Can you think about something told to you that made you lose faith in yourself?

2. What is one thing that you would love to do but are holding back because of fear? It can be anything. Do not think of the reasons why you cannot achieve it. Write it down on a piece of paper with precise details. Then read it aloud and imagine yourself doing what you love.

3. When we get hurt by loved ones we tend to build hate and resentment in our hearts. This is not healthy because it deprives us of our own happiness. Forgiving is evolving. Who should you forgive this very moment?

BIOGRAPHY

Nuvia Yesenia was born in Denver, Colorado. After her parents divorced, she moved to Jalisco, Mexico, with her mother and grandparents. Later, she and her mother relocated in Chicago, Illinois. Nuvia currently works as an interpreter for an Illinois State Program called Early intervention. She provides interpretation services for the families and therapists she works with. Behind her professional job is a creative soul who loves to write songs, play the drums, record music or motivational videos on YouTube, and write fascinating stories. Since she was a child, she idolized the pop/rock singer Gloria Trevi. Her dream was for one day to become a singer just like her. She is currently pursuing her bachelor's degree in English in hopes of one day working for *National Geographic Magazine* as an editor. She is the author of *My New Veganning,* and co-author of an amazing book called Hispanic Stars Rising. She has also published her first book in Spanish called *UNA NOTA EN BLANCO.* Nuvia has recorded several of the songs she wrote in a professional studio and continues to expand her music skills and knowledge.

Nuvia Yesenia
Email: nuviayeseniawrites@gmail.com
IG: nuvia_yesenia_writes
Blog Website: https://www.
theessenceofagoddess.org/

Rochelle Ceballos

"It's a blessing to be a blessing."

One of my favorite parts about our heritage is the importance of family. Outside of God, it is the foundation to my success. Although life's lessons weren't always preached as "this will make you successful," the principles I learned from my family helped equip me with the tools necessary to succeed in life, so that I could live out my God given purpose.

THE FOUNDATION

My Grandma Ceballos showed me love in such a graceful way. My Grandpa Ceballos spoiled me to another level and made me feel like the most loved woman in the world. He also showed me the importance of legacy. My Grandma Torres taught me the importance of being proud of who you are and to always be a good listener. My Grandpa Torres showed me the power of connection with others and that strangers can actually be your friends.

My *tios* and *tias* showed the importance of being supportive and being there for your family, through thick and thin.

And of course, my parents. They are it all. I followed their lead. Their example. They always spoke life into my life. They opened up my eyes when it came to entrepreneurship and supported me along the journey.

When I was a pre-teen, I played soccer and I loved it! I was a great athlete too. I remember coming home one day after a game and telling my dad, "Dad! I made 3 goals today." He looked at me and said, "That's it? I want 5." I'm not going to lie. I was kind of mad. "Why can't he just be happy like the other dads?" I said to myself. Then, I went back to my day, like any other pre-teen would. The next soccer game, I remember, I scored another 3 goals, but the game wasn't over yet, and I went for more (remembering what my dad had said). And guess what? I scored more than 3. I finished the game with 5 goals! I couldn't believe it! In my mind, 5 goals were impossible!

That day, I learned that nothing was impossible. My dad never let me get excited about doing "good." He taught me that the Ceballos were great and that we should always aim for more than just "good."

There were times when I thought it was unfair, but now, I'm so grateful! My dad instilled inside of me, to never settle and to always go above and beyond.

My mom, she is truly something special. What I love about my mom is she never made it easy for us. In childhood, I was like, "why is she like this?" I remember when I was in Girl Scouts and, of course, I wanted to sell the most cookies. When I told her that, I was hoping that she would help me win, by taking my order sheet to work and asking the other moms to buy from me. Instead, she made me go, door to door, to different people's houses, to get the order from them personally. "But, mom, I'm scared." (And secretly, I wanted to win the easy way). Instead of making it easy for me, she told me that by the third house, it would get easier. And, guess what? She was right!

I don't remember if I won that year in Girl Scouts, but I do remember that my mom taught me how to overcome my fears and to never let being "scared" stop me from accomplishing my goals. She showed me the power of putting in the work necessary to succeed and now in life, I no longer desire the "easy way."

OVERNIGHT SUCCESS?

I started my first business at the age of 26 in the online world. I had no idea what I was doing, I just knew it was my calling. I knew that God had created me for impact and as I found my calling, I was led to entrepreneurship.

I would love to tell you that I was an overnight success. That I woke up one day, and BAM I was making money in my sleep and that everything was flowing, but it wasn't. My first years of entrepreneurship were rough, I didn't make any money. I laugh about it now, but then, it was frustrating. I often sent up prayers, asking God, "why?" I was putting in the work, the hours, I even had lots of passion, but nothing seemed to connect.

What I didn't realize is that, although I wasn't making all the money in the world, I was gaining something that is very important, on your journey to success and in entrepreneurship, "experience" I was becoming a master in the online space and I didn't even realize it.

Wise words from my dad, "The only difference between successful people and unsuccessful people is that one quits and the other one keeps going and gains experience."

So although the struggle was real, instead of quitting, I stayed focused on the prize, and did not give up.

WHAT DOES SUCCESS MEAN TO YOU?

Success looks different, to everyone. I will share with you what I did to become successful, but for this to happen in your life, it's so important that you define what success is in your life. It's very hard to attain anything in life if you don't know what you want.

Is success financial freedom to you? Is success making a certain amount of money? Is success happiness? Is success being able to travel wherever you desire? Is success more time with your family?

In my early 20s, I attempted to be successful in other people's eyes, instead of my own. Due to this mindset, I struggled. I wasn't happy. Nothing seemed to fulfill me. After I let go of attempting to impress others, I realized that I had no idea what I wanted in my own life. It wasn't until I sat down and thought about what I wanted in life and what success meant to me, when I started to feel fulfilled and aligned.

Success to me is freedom. Freedom to travel the world and experience its many cultures. I envision laughing with my family, creating incredible memories, where money is never an issue. Success means alignment with God and my purpose. It's making my family proud and also leaving a powerful legacy. A legacy that will make an impact on future generations.

Knowing what success means to me, helped me pursue it. It gave me reason to wake up every day and go after it. It helped me push through the tough days. The tough days were worth it because I knew what was coming.

USE YOUR GOD GIVEN TALENTS

I believe that each of us are given gifts during our time on earth and it's up to us to share them with the world, to create impact.

Although some of us may have similar gifts, no one can execute your gift, like you can. You were created, unique, on purpose.

Even us, as Latinas, have a unique gift that we can offer to this world. It most definitely unites each of us, but at the same time, each of us share our heritage in a different way, in a unique way. I call this, your superpower, because no one can be YOU like YOU can.

Some of us have the gift of speaking. Others have a gift of caregiving. Others have a gift of teaching, etc. Each gift that we have, is necessary, for the greater good of this world. It's all about tapping into that gift, owning that gift, and sharing that gift with the world.

IT'S A BLESSING TO BE A BLESSING

A key to success is to not focus on the self, but to focus on impact.. Knowing your gift, your purpose, is great, but if you do not use it, if you hold it inside of you, the world will never experience it.

As I run my business and help others pursue their God-given purpose, I teach people the mindset of blessing others. Instead of thinking "I want more money for me, I'm doing this for myself, etc.," it's important to look at life and business in a way of "how can I bless someone else with my product, service, and/or message with the world?" This mindset will not only bless others, it will bless your life as well.

I learned this principle from the Bible, "give and it will be given to you." I always looked at it in a monetary way. "If I give more money, I'll get more money?" But, what I learned is that, yes, this scripture can be monetarily, but also, in so many other ways.

Give (bless) others with your time. Although you may think that giving someone your time will only be beneficial for them, you'll find that that time will absolutely bless you as well.

Give (bless) others with your wisdom. Giving your wisdom freely, will bless your life. As a coach and a mentor, when I see others succeed quicker due to the wisdom I was able to bless them with, my heart lights up. I know, yours will too.

Bless others with love. The world needs more of this. It's something we don't see as much and when you share a loving spirit with others, sometimes, they will be shocked, but you will impact their life in a great way.

There are many other ways to bless others, but these are just a few. I go, throughout my days, thinking, "how can I bless others" and because of that mindset, I do believe I have been able to find a certain level of success and influence in my life.

PUTTING IT ALL TOGETHER

I am, by no means, the most talented person in the world. I do not have a college degree, I was not a straight A student in high school; however, I have been able to excel in taking action on the principles I've learned in life. Whether it was what my grandparents taught me early on, what my parents continue to show me daily, or what I read in the Bible or other mentorship I receive.

I am living proof that anyone can accomplish its dreams and purpose if taken seriously. I take mine seriously, I think about the people who could be missing out because I decided to settle on life and it's in those moments, where I continue to push through, regardless of how I feel.

Will the journey be easy? No. Will it be worth it? Absolutely!

YOU ARE A BLESSING

I want you to know, the person reading these pages, right now, that you are a blessing to this world. Your gifts, your purpose, is necessary and my prayer is that you live out that purpose.

This world will try to get you to forget about impact. There will be times when you will say, "it's easier to go a different route," but you were created for more. You are a powerful Latina, who is created for impact. Own who you are. Don't let anyone stop you or tell you differently.

When you are struggling, remind yourself, where you came from, who you are fighting for, and also, look ahead to the future. Look at the impact you will make, if you keep going, regardless of how hard it may seem. Your dreams are worth fighting for. Your dreams will change lives. They will bless so many others.

With love,
Rochelle Ceballos

REFLECTION QUESTIONS

1. What does success mean to you?

2. What are some of your God-given talents and how are you using them?

3. Why are you striving for success?

BIOGRAPHY

Rochelle Ceballos started her entrepreneurial career at the age of 26. She builds online businesses and is passionate about helping others find their purpose and gain financial literacy.

From a young age, Rochelle showed endless leadership abilities, but it wasn't until her late 20s, where she realized her calling and her purpose. Rochelle utilized the era of the internet and has been able to make over 6 figures helping people, online through social media platforms like Instagram, Facebook, and Tik Tok.

With this skillset and the passion to help others win, she has helped multiple people, leave their corporate America job and pursue entrepreneurship full time.

Her lifelong goal is to help as many people as possible gain financial freedom, so that they can live a life they love and deserve.

Rochelle Ceballos
info@rochelleceballos.com
instagram.com/rochelleceballos
facebook.com/rochelle.ceballos
twitter.com/urfavrochell

Sandra L. Diaz

"Life is 10% what happens to you and 90% how you react to it"
—Charles Swindoll

They say, "Never look back because you are not going that way." Yet, sometimes, it is necessary so you can remember a lesson, appreciate what you have and/or remain humble. Memories or feelings come back to you throughout your life. And you recall them as good or bad. When it is a good memory, you smile and relive a happy moment, but when it is bad, you have to get rid of that thought immediately. As I think about my experiences, I am grateful for everything.

STATISTICS

At the age of 15, I entered the statistics I never wanted to join: a young pregnant Latina. I was an honor student that had just experienced great junior high school years away from the neighborhood magnet school. However, I had to return to my neighborhood to finish school because I was the oldest of five children, and my parents worked double shifts at paper companies or factories. We grew up independent, yet limited as to the things we could do, the places we could go, and how far we could dream of. It was hard to study and learn of all the great industries and careers and feel that, for some reason, they were unreachable.

I faced a hard choice to make: enter an alternative high school for pregnant girls, get on welfare, drop out of school and care for my baby, or continue attending school and graduate anyway. This is where my memories take me. I believe I could not have asked for better mentors, loving teachers, administrators and friends. Benito Juarez High School could not have taught me better lessons: to see what it is like to live in rough socio-economic conditions to understand what other people are going through.

From school, I remember an economics teacher, Mr. Donovan, who did great things that went unnoticed by many. Back then, there were daily newspapers, we all gave him a dollar to buy a stock and watched how it did in the market. He also brought in the Junior Achievement program, where a banker went in to provide financial education. He talked about checking and the importance of saving for the future. Later, that VP banker would become one of my dearest mentors at my first job. I think this program needs to come back to school, maybe with fewer contents like credit. What is credit? How do you build and destroy credit? What can you use it for? Why is it important? This is one of the projects I hope to work on soon and help bring financial literacy to our young community.

PIVOTING

I think my first time at McDonald's was when I was nine. We never ordered pizza, and God forbid if you asked for it because there was plenty of rice and beans to eat at home. (Which is the true story why I love my *frijoles*!) The first place I took my son when he was able to ask for something was McDonald's. It is every child's dream! Moreover, I was the cool mom that let him open up his toys before he ate. Yet, we also had a big challenge called Toys R Us on Rockwell, as I could not afford the toys he wanted. I had two jobs because my parents were against me getting on public aid, and I barely made ends meet. I struggled for commuting, or otherwise I risked being fired. I got both jobs through high school friends. One told me about a neighborhood program that helped find a job for students doing well at school. And, I got my first job at a bank. Although I worked only a few hours because of school schedules, in summer, they gave me more hours. The second job was a late shift at a big grocery store where some friends worked. That was truly scary because I had to run through the UIC area where there were lots of homeless and drug addicts staying at the abandoned facilities. Those times were so appalling that I sometimes cried. Anyway, I needed to support my son.

As time went by, I was able to focus on the banking job that led me into my career. I became a commercial loan processor and I helped organize our banks networking events, uniting and generating businesses. I am so thankful for the Presidents, Vice Presidents, Managers of that bank who taught me how to dress professionally, how to speak professionally (code switching, as we would call it now), and how to build a network and keep it. They were also huge on customer service and, as a community bank, everyone from the receptionist to the top officer cared for the clients as family. As I learned about the importance of families' financial health, I do my best to be as informative and caring as possible. I feel that it is a big responsibility as a real estate professional to properly educate and guide clients along.

At the age of 20, I got married, I bought my house at 21 and I had my second child at 27. This second pregnancy was different. I had to go through a fertility treatment. Those were very sad times. I felt like I had done everything right. I had a husband, a great career, a house; I mean, I was more than ready! Answering the question, "When are you having a baby?" was quite heartbreaking and unbearable. However, thank God, I was able to have him and my son was happy with his little brother. For some time, everything was great, but then, we went through the 2008 market crash. We lost our home and I wanted to keep my real estate career afloat. Those were undeniably learning times. I learned to change, helped translate court documents, learned about property taxes, tax exemptions, and tax appeals. I did anything I could to help and make a little more money to make it through. Eventually, I had to accept a slight career transformation to work for the WIC (Women, Infant and Children) program as an intake clerk. I always wanted to work for a non-profit or community organization, so it was perfect as my son attended the Gad Hill Program just above my job. There, I could see the importance of community programs and the need to fight for them, too. I met some great program directors as well as dietitians, and I really enjoyed the experience of serving the community. Besides, you get to see babies, and then, watch them grow up.

EPIPHANY

I took a break from work to go back to study. At first, I thought I was too old, but then I found a great diversity in ages and cultures, and it was great. DeVry University did help me identify my skills. I enrolled for Business Administration focused on Project Management. That, my friends, would lead me to my current position as an Operations Manager to the number one Latino real estate team in Illinois. When I worked for the bank at the beginning of my career, I always wanted to work for the Re/Max office I am right now: Re/Max Partners. I heard about the power of the mind. It is amazing what happens when you put it out in the Universe. When I started to work for my current mentor, he was creating a team. He went through the organization of the operations and shared his vision and mission for his team. As we grew, everything else did. We now own two franchises and have expanded our business! Seeing a project succeed, when you have been part of it since the beginning, is one of the best feelings for me, as a project manager and a team member.

One of the most important requirements when a team member joins is to highlight the importance of community services and volunteer work. We believe in giving back to the communities not only monetary support but also time. Considering our team like family helps our members be happy to help, and it is also a great example to our children and families. We struggle together, learn together, grow together and love one another.

GO BACK TO WHERE YOUR HEART IS

A few years ago, I felt the need to go back to my community in Pilsen to give back, help fundraise, volunteer, or provide assistance, as needed. Looking back, I do not think I would have become the person I am if I had not overcome the obstacles that others and I put in my way. I learned to work hard, to be accountable, and to become a mother and a caring person. I am grateful to understand people, the way others understood me during difficult times. When I was pregnant, people asked me if I needed clothes or baby stuff. Especially, the people from Dvorak Park where I started my volunteer work.

This year I was given the opportunity to run for Alderwoman in my hometown, and I believe that was the highlight of my career. All my family and friends were out supporting me, and my sons could not be prouder. It was like the result of all my previous work, and although I did not win, I know there were many people and other women following me and looking up to me. As I do not have any daughters, I was glad to see my nieces and Goddaughters look up to me. Sometimes we do not really know who we are inspiring and being able to be a role model is a big part of the decisions and the work I include in my projects. After the election, I was offered the position of Chair Lady to the Board of Directors of Break the Silence Foundation, which is an organization to help victims of domestic violence put back together by empowering them to become self-sufficient and productive in the communities. We even have a group of surgeons that help reconstruct the victims' faces. I look forward to giving the foundation all the support I can to continue with the mission and save more lives.

The outbreak of COVID-19 last year was definitely a life-changing experience for many. I feel that we went through every existing emotion and, in my case, as a team leader, I needed to help the team get through it. When I get scared or feel threatened, I go into survival mode and I face adversity like a buffalo. But this time was different, it was not only about my life, it was about everyone else around me. So, I read as much as I could, I prayed as hard as I could, and I listened to every webinar from some of the top motivational speakers. I needed to be positive, more empathetic, and more loving. Leadership comes with great responsibility, thus, you must consistently develop the tools necessary to help yourself and the others. Everyone is a leader, whether at home or elsewhere. We just have to step up to the challenges we come across.

Life is full of experiences that will head for the direction in which you are meant to be. I have learned that you always have to adapt to changes and be prepared for the opportunities that arise. Always be confident to move forward, no matter you succeed or not, the result will always be positive. I hope you enjoy your ride, accept the trials and tribulations, and grow to become the special person you are meant to be.

REFLECTION QUESTIONS

1. How do you show that you are responsible for your life?

2. Who sets the highest expectations for you? Are you living up to them?

3. Who sets the highest expectations for you? Are you living up to them?

BIOGRAPHY

As a banking sector professional since she was seventeen, Sandra learned early how to leverage her ability to connect with others to become a way of communications at all levels of the banking industry. Today, she continues to serve the community as an advocate for equity in housing practices. She strives to ensure our industry always provides the community with clear information. Her passion is rooted from community building and pride, where she makes sure to invest time and funding to cultural causes, local non-profits, the arts, and public spaces. She is grateful to deal with many Berwyn residents devoted to community-wide events, such as the annual Mariachi 5k of North Berwyn Park District, The Annual Day of the Dead, Christmas Toy Drive, Easter, Children's Day events, and many others.

She is a mother, a daughter, a sister, a realtor and a team builder at *RE/MAX Partners*. As the oldest of five siblings, she knows what it takes to create the environment needed to come together. She is there every step of the way, from beginning to end, whether it is organizing an event, volunteering, or fundraising for a cause. Most recently, she became Chair Lady of the board of directors for Break the Silence Foundation, a member of Berwyn Women in Business and Dvorak Park Advisory Council.

Sandra L. Diaz
Operations Manager/Broker
Team Luis Ortiz
Office: 708-387-3149
Cell: 773-571-0411
remax.sandrad@gmail.com

María Rodolfa Gómez Rodriguez

"Just as the water reflects the stars and the moon,
the body reflects the mind and the soul" - Rumi

THE BEGINNING

I was born in a small town, where the school system had little to offer. Thus, when I was nine, I had the hard task to decide whether to stay sheltered by my parents, and mainly within the loving sanctuary of my grandparents' home, or to live far from them in order to study. I still remember Sunday afternoons when I took the van back to school after enjoying a family weekend, the hum of the old engine deafened my cry that lasted the whole journey. Now, when I think about it, I could not refrain that instinct; but I also knew that my grandmother's saying was true, "achieving my dreams and enjoying comforts are apples from different baskets."

Learning became my favorite sport, and even with undiagnosed dyslexia, I managed to attain a bachelor's degree in Psychology, then a master's degree and different specialized diplomas. In the summer of 2000, everything seemed fabulous,

I was finishing my PhD in Existential Psychotherapy with honors, which meant an unquestionable success for me and a fair compensation for so many tears shed over living alone. Although I found wonderful angels on my way who opened their homes and hearts to me, deep down, I knew that I did not belong there, and that undoubtedly hurt a lot leaving deep marks in life.

School assignments and heavy office workload caught most of my attention; my professional expertise was the queen of the cake and I felt successful.

THE DARK NIGHT OF MY SOUL

When I was at college, I met a boy whom I married, and we had a beautiful daughter. I believed our relationship was good and funny; but after the hot summer, the terribly cold winter arrived. Of course, it was not so cold, as I still lived in Puerto Vallarta, a beautiful coast city where the lowest temperature can reach 60 °F, but at that time, I felt I was frozen cold. The atmosphere was so dense that I found it difficult to breathe. As the relationship with my partner was falling apart, I changed from fury to sadness in a second, I did not know how or what to do. Between emotional comings and goings, it took us almost four years to get out, a rather long agony for all of us, as my little girl's teenage years went by. She had no choice but to mature to support her parents who had become two impossible teenagers.

Finally, the obvious occurred: we put an end to our relationship and I was left emotionally devastated, not only because of the breakup, but also because of all the collateral losses that came with it. In the course of those twenty-one years of marriage, I had created very solid relationships with his family. My own family with a *macho* vision did not approve of my divorce, so that bond was shattered, as well. Several friends did not know which side to take, either. My daughter started her professional career in another city, so she moved away from me, which pushed me into a deep sorrow.

As a professional, I received patients with the same problems I was going through, and my inner self did not hesitate to judge me in the worst way. I told myself how dishonest it was to be in front of another person who was looking for my help, when I had been unable to move forward from my own relationship. I was afraid that my patients would realize what I was experiencing, and for the first time, I regretted and felt ashamed of having chosen that profession and, I cursed everybody, even God.

Soon I found myself in a bottomless and shapeless well. My fear seemed to swallow my bowels and to leave me hollow inside, where the slightest gust of wind could hurt me. I felt old, ugly, clumsy and even unable to make ends meet. My heart seemed to be cracking inside; sometimes it did not move at all, and on some other occasions, it was beating so hard that I felt it was outside my body. I started thinking that it was better to die than to live, and that thought made me realize that I had to do something and urgently.

MY ESCAPE

I could not take it anymore, and I ran away. I applied as a volunteer to teach how to prepare Mexican food in the Peruvian mountains. I arrived there three months before the vacancy opened. The warmth of the Peruvians, the spectacular landscapes and the company of other wonderful beings slowly healed my soul. As I still could not stay in the camp, several times a week, I went with the health caravan to serve the most unwelcoming but beautiful places in the mountains of Cusco. One of the places we visited was also a women's prison, where I met Sofia (so-called for identity protection). She was imprisoned for committing filicide. Actually, she was a suicidal girl, with a high degree of guilt with an anxiety crisis, for which she was desperately seeking to end her life. That led her to engage in behaviors that others considered extremely dangerous. She was kept in a separate cell and her exits to the patio were restricted. As I had nothing to do, little by little, I got closer to her, and gained her trust, until she allowed me to do a psychotherapeutic work with her. That was one of the best experiences I have undergone as a transpersonal psychologist. I clearly learned about the existence of other worlds and other dimensions (anyway, that will be the subject of another chapter). Sofia significantly changed her behavior. She stopped attacking herself and others all of a sudden.

THE MIRACLE

Priest Nicanor asked to speak to me. (The Father, as we all told him, is an extraordinary being, who is not only in charge of his parish, but he is also a great leader who receives people from different corners of the world, especially from Europe and Japan, to support the most forgotten communities in the mountains and

Cusco.) "Maria, you have accomplished a miracle with Sofia!" The father told me very excited. Surprised by his thankfulness, I confessed that I was a psychotherapist and that what I did was a Gestalt psychotherapy job, which was not really a miracle. I saw how his cute face was transformed... while a long silence surrounded us both. The tension was so strong that it seemed to be burning me. Finally, he uttered the words, "What's that?" With all the nervousness built up in the silence, I tried to explain. With an angry voice, he asked me, "Why didn't you tell me? You know the need for this service in the community and you want to teach us how to prepare Mexican food?" I explained what I was going through: my divorce and my contradiction of being a psychotherapist, which was the real reason for being there. With a firm and even severe voice, he told me, "What you are doing, girl, is fleeing!" (I felt a bucket of cold water fell on me, it was a few days before the place to stay for six months was available.)

As much as I tried to defend myself and to make him change his mind, I failed. Finally, the loving Priest returned and told me, "You can't run away from your own story, sooner or later it will catch up with you. My house's doors are always open for you, but you need to return to your country and your city, face your ghosts and rescue the extraordinary psychologist from inside. And, when you feel worthy of the wonderful woman you are, come back. I will be waiting for you and you will have a place in the community you choose, or right here at the Polyclinic." That was the end of conversation that day. The ghosts reappeared in my mind, the atmosphere started to become thicker, but there also appeared some unexplainable bursts of joy.

Meanwhile, the Priest started organizing my farewell, and it would definitely include Mexican food prepared by me. That is when I realized that I had never prepared the nixtamal. I desperately called my mother to get the recipe, and with blistered hands from trying to clean the corn, I managed to prepare the dough for tacos and slightly hard quesadillas, and a pozole with corn that never popped up. A very emotional farewell filled me with confidence for what I had to face. My luggage was full of gratitude, love and new dreams to fulfill. I also found out that they had never been interested in my proposal of Mexican food. They only accepted me because it was the first time that a Mexican woman wanted to participate, and I confessed to them what was obvious: "that I did not know how to prepare Mexican food."

BACK HOME

The Priest seemed to guess my thoughts, as when I decided to go back, I thought, "Well, I'm going to Guadalajara" and, at that same moment, he said, "Go to the same city, and if possible, to the same office." So I quietly returned home.

While I was unpacking the aroma of Peru, I sat on my bed and everything seemed so strange. It was the same, but at the same time, it was not. Nothing had changed but everything looked different. Suddenly, I realized that I had changed. I left broken, with my soul in pieces and I came back accompanied by myself. Soon, I faced the daily routine of my life, but with a renewed look, very strong to face the challenges that I did not remember having before. I learned that the greatest hell was not outside but inside me. The way I was feeling, my daily thoughts, could have opened ravines where there were only a few ditches.

I could also separate myself from the victim who hurt me so much. Slowly, I accepted that I had been a partner in a damaged relationship, and I rediscovered my power by stopping the game at the exact moment I chose to do it. I am much more than my circumstances, and much more than my emotional condition, I knew that I could get out of this feeling at will, and I found it fascinating, which became my legacy to share with others.

My listening of and company to my patients became more refined and warmer, clearly recognizing my limitations and their expertise in their own life.

I know this is not the end of the story. I have faced and will face many new challenges in my life. I also understood that getting down to hell and being able to come out has left me great learnings, one of the biggest is that I AM NOT going to die for that. At the end of the tunnel, there is always a light waiting. It depends on us to go through it, or to stay to live in the dungeon. I would be untruthful if I told you that I have not gone back to hell. I just want to tell you that I can get out faster and ask for help sooner.

I still think that life is a wonderful adventure where we are constantly re-writing the script, as co-authors with him/her, the creator of the universe.

Enjoy it, it will come to an end...

Thanks.

REFLECTION QUESTIONS

1. Have you ever felt that life turned against you?

2. How did you manage to get out of there?

3. Which learnings have you acquired? Do not let them vanish in you, because you pay with your life for them.

BIOGRAPHY

María Rodolfa is in love with life. She is the mother of Naiat and grandmother of Sebastian and Marcelo. She works as a psychotherapist and coach. She is the director of CAPCI Pto. Vallarta (Center for Psychological Attention and Comprehensive Training). She has taught different undergraduate courses, she has worked as a teacher in different universities and institutes in courses to attain bachelor's, master's, and PhD degrees. She has earned more than 30 years of experience as a psychotherapist.

She was the chairperson of the Asociación de Terapeutas de Danza y Movimiento Gloria Simcha Ruben and achieved the most successful international congress of this association.

She is a writer, author of the book *Coaching para la prosperidad* and *Los cuentos de María, metáforas psicoterapéuticas.* She co-authored the book *Coaching educativo y transpersonal.*

Her educational background includes a BA in Educational Psychology, a Master's in Gestalt Psychotherapy, a PhD in Existential Psychotherapies, and specializations in Dance therapy, NLP, Ericksonian Hypnosis, and Family Psychotherapy.

As Maria is interested in perennial psychology, she has traveled to different parts of Mexico and around the world to live and learn about these experiences.

María Rodolfa Gómez Rodríguez
Maryrodo.gomez@gmail.com
Tel: (52) 3223031288
YouTube: maria rodolfa gomez
Facebook: Maria Rodolfa

Priscilla Guasso

"Rejection is temporary, giving up makes it permanent."

When I was a child, collecting rocks was one of my favorite pastimes. I could spend hours outside searching for the perfect rock to call my own. I was fascinated at how most rocks could look so ordinary, dull, and unassuming; yet after putting them through a few weeks in a grinding rock tumbler, they become smooth, colorful, and beautiful. This "grind" it seems, is the perfect metaphor to the many questions and experiences that I have wrestled with throughout my life's journey:

- *What's my purpose?*
- *What if I can't do it, or I fail?*
- *Am I enough?*
- *Who am I to lead?*
- *What legacy will I leave behind?*

Like the craftsman polishing and cutting a diamond in the rough into a beautiful stone, what if our life is the result of molding and polishing our edges through everyday pressures and grinds to later shine from within? There is a popular quote that says, "pressure creates diamonds," but when things get really tough how many of us question ourselves how much more "pressure" can we truly take? Our journey can often feel dark when we are strained, but I encourage you to join me in holding tight to hope and believing that life's challenges are polishing us for something greater ahead.

LIVE INTENTIONALLY AND BECOME *EXTRA*-ORDINARY

As I approach another birthday, I cannot help but reflect on where I'm spending my time, what I'm doing, and whom I'm around. Why, you might ask? Because someone wise once told me, *"dime con quién andas y te diré quién eres,"* meaning "you will be judged by the company you keep." As the years go by, this saying resonates even stronger with me. It is so easy to get caught up in the whirlwind around us, getting lost in the latest and greatest on social media; all to realize our true focus should be on investing in our own journey, polishing our craft and letting our actions lead to results. Much easier said than done, right?

The pressures of my 37 years of life made me think hard about the abovementioned questions and our COVID-19 pandemic was a catalyst that cemented my desire to focus on my life, where I am and where I'm going. I left the comfort of a well-paying job, leaned into my interests of building a thriving professional community called Latinas In HR™, published a beautiful book titled Latinas Rising Up In HR © and pursued a new opportunity: focusing on my financial, spiritual, physical and mental health. This required me to confront my own pressures and insecurities and convince myself I was ready to lead a group of amazing women, swim in uncharted waters, and create a niche no one in Human Resources (HR) had previously explored before.

I prepared my head and heart to connect with hundreds of fascinating, accomplished, and phenomenal women in HR, all of whom had an inspiring story to share. As I did this, I needed to remind myself every day that I could achieve my ambitions, but it would require I push out any negativity and hold tight to the hope and belief that we *all* have the power to make a big change… starting with myself. It was time that Latina leadership in HR received greater visibility, and what better time than the present to embark on something magical that had never been done before.

There are still days I need to stop, reflect, and celebrate this dream I achieved. It is true, no victory is achieved alone, but the biggest hurdle for me was having the courage to believe I'm extra-ordinary and that I had to make the first move. I spent five years sitting on the idea of building this phenomenal community of Latinas In HR™ and with the extraordinary support around me, my book Latinas Rising Up In HR© was born. Regardless of all the dreams I continue to go after, do not be fooled, I still fight the negative thoughts that creep in from time to time. It is scary and thrilling to feel like you are building the plane as you fly it. At the end of the day, my greatest rewards are seeing how many lives we continue to touch with the work we do (like our two HR scholarships), and hearing from many Latinas in HR at all levels share, "I finally feel seen and supported."

I encourage you to dig deep, do the work to convince yourself, and believe *you are extra*-ordinary as well. *Believe and act as if!* As you sail through your own journey, you will slowly find yourself supported by those that believe in your light; hold those people close and invite them to live your journey with you by sharing your dreams and worries. I continue to work on my affirmations every day, as I share my vulnerabilities. Any pressures or defining moments you endure in life are what shape and set you apart to become the great warrior, *la guerrera*, you are and will continue to grow into. Believing you're *extra*-ordinary should not happen only once; it is a constant mindset and requires training before going into the battlefield.

It is in these moments I hear God's soft whisper saying, *"Trust me. I have given you gifts, now use them."* It is confronting your fears, choosing to believe in something greater and *always taking a chance on you.* Throughout my career I've seen fear defined in two ways: **F**orget **E**verything **A**nd **R**un or **F**ace **E**verything **A**nd **R**ise. As nerve-wrecking or unclear as some days may feel, I choose to face everything and rise while reminding others to do so too. Remember, *rejection is temporary, giving up makes it permanent.* The more that we choose to give into our fears, the more we are depriving ourselves of our potential growth and light, which we can shine on others.

SMOOTHING OUT THE EDGES

Months following the success of my book and creation of a community, I discovered we were expecting a child. After two years and two miscarriages, I felt on top of the world and ready to embark on this next chapter with my husband. Having been in this place before, I would be lying if I didn't admit I was terrified. I tried my hardest not to worry and remain hopeful, but I knew nothing was guaranteed. The morning I was to fly back home from a family trip, I experienced my third miscarriage; I was devastated. My worst fear had come back and all the feelings I worked so hard to process a year earlier were front and center in my life again. As I laid in bed with my sister crying and processing, my phone rang and I remember my sister asking, *"are you sure you want to take that call right now?"*

For whatever reason I did, and it was the voice of a recruiter offering me the very position I was focusing on getting so intensely months earlier. I was so perplexed and shocked that part of me could not help but think that this was some sort of sign from God, *but a sign of what?* I was still sniffling when I answered the phone and pretended to be sick, as I was barely able to speak a word through the tsunami of tears. Then, an hour went by, and I received news that a corporation I had been looking forward to collaborating with for my Latinas In HR™ community, was officially interested in moving ahead. My heart could barely withstand all the emotions from these three hours. My exact thoughts were *"What is happening here God? What the heck are you doing up there?"*

Over the next few weeks my heart continued to shatter, as loved ones would try to console me, asking me what the doctor's opinion was regarding the reason this happened. While I know their heart was in the right place, I really disliked this question because there is no exact rhyme or reason for why a miscarriage happens. Although they are generally taboo subjects, miscarriages are *very* common. I later learned many women in my life had experienced one themselves. According to the *March of Dimes* organization, 10-15% of women suffer a miscarriage. Despite this, do not let a miscarriage deflate your dreams. Going through a miscarriage does not mean you will never get pregnant.

Even though the rock tumbler of life continued polishing my existence with this tragic event, all I wanted to do was remain a dull rock- I wanted to hide deep in the Earth, alone in my thoughts and not think of any silver linings. This time though, before heading down to hide, I shared with a few family and friends what I was going through. This is very contrary to who I am. Previously, nobody would have ever known what was really going on with me, because my smile never cracked. I was determined to change, because like everyone, I am human and was not going to hide behind a mask any longer. I shared with my close community how I did not feel like talking, but welcomed texting, since that felt easier to do. I allowed myself space to grieve again.

This time, however, I was surrounded by an extremely large community: my amazing co-authors from <u>Latinas Rising Up In HR</u> © constantly encouraged me, the board from Fig Factor Foundation extended grace and lifted me up as I briefly disconnected from a newly appointed board seat, my amazing family prayed for us daily, and my husband remained by my side comforting me through the physical and emotional pain. After a few weeks of allowing my mind, body, and soul to heal, I slowly came back up for air holding onto the belief that God was carrying us through this storm. While I wish this on no one, we all need to experience the journey of living to become who we are meant to be. No matter what life-changing event you are going through, my desire is that you give yourself space to break down to later have greater capacity to continue working towards achieving your own greatness.

BOLD STEPS AND AN EVOLVING JOURNEY

A recurring theme that has been key to my evolving journey is no matter what the challenge is- be it personal or professional- taking that first step requires boldness. The mere fact you were born is a miracle and already proves you are *extra*-ordinary. Any small change could have caused you to not to exist as you are today, from how your parents met, to your conception, and all that you experienced from childhood to adulthood. Tonight, before you fall asleep, I invite you to place your hand over your heart and take a minute to feel your heartbeat. Take a bold step to think of an affirmation for you that will combat any negative talk in your mind.

In my case, it would sound something like, *"Priscilla, you're fearless. You always find a way to get things done and inject a powerful uplifting energy to those around you. Fearlessly let your light shine bright."* Take this bold first step with me. Push the negative pressures out and pull in people that lift you up- people that challenge you, celebrate you, support you and encourage you to think *"what if this really works out?"* We are living a time in history with many firsts happening all around us and the reality is it's easier to give up. We need you to believe you're *extra*-ordinary. You can and will be the ripple effect of change amongst your family, friends, and our community. Without a doubt you will feel the pressure, but just like the rocks I collected when I was a child, by taking small, bold steps forward, over time your reward will be the sparkle within you shining even brighter than you could have ever imagined.

REFLECTION QUESTIONS

1. What is stopping you from feeling extra-ordinary?

2. What affirmation do you need to hear, believe, or act out?

    - Write it down: I AM _____

3. What will be your next three, small, yet bold steps?

    1._____ 2._____ 3._____

BIOGRAPHY

Based in both Chicago and Miami, Priscilla Guasso thrives in leading human resources teams focused on all areas of the employee life cycle: talent acquisition, mobility, talent development, succession planning, performance management, employee relations, global diversity, equity and inclusion, and overall company culture. Her fifteen plus years of experience expands to HR in the US, Latin America, Caribbean, UK and Canada, in hospitality, healthcare and currently in the technology industry.

She enjoys coaching others to invest in their leadership skills as entrepreneurs, and in the corporate, nonprofit and government sectors. As Amazon's Best-Selling Author of <u>Latinas Rising Up In HR©</u> and Founder of Latinas In HR™ her community is focused on one purpose: *sharing keys of knowledge and success to O-P-E-N doors of unlimited possibilities!*

Priscilla holds a BSc in Business Administration with a concentration in Marketing from the University of Illinois, Urbana/Champaign. Recognized as *Negocios Now* 2020 Latinos 40 Under 40, she proudly serves as a board member for the Fig Factor Foundation. She is a contributing speaker in the 2021 LATINA Talks Global Tour, an inspiration agent for Young Latina Day (April 11th) and proud member of: HRHotseat, Hispanic Star Miami, Society of Human Resources Management (SHRM), The Latinista and previous board member of: National Hispanic Corporate Council (NHCC), Mujeres de HACE Chicago and Latino/Latina Alumni Association for University of Illinois. She thoroughly enjoys traveling to different countries with her husband, Jorge, soaking up the sun in warmer climates.

Priscilla Guasso
HR Leader
Author, Latinas Rising Up In HR©
Founder, Latinas In HR™
Let's connect: www.LinkedIn.com/in/
PriscillaGuasso
Priscilla@LatinasRisingUpInHR.com
www.LatinasRisingUpInHR.com
@PriscillaGuasso @LatinasInHR

Behati Hart

"Forgiveness reveals the dwelling place of God within us"
- Iyanla Vanzant

I'm an Afro-Latina from the South Side of Chicago, Illinois. My mother, only 14 years old at the time, shared with me that I was the result of her rape. As a mother of two amazing young women, I would sometimes imagine the pain and anger my grandfather must have felt when he learned his young daughter was violated. My mother told me about her choice to keep me and extend her grace to forgive my biological father. He was a 20+ year old, African-American man and lived in the same apartment complex as my mother and grandfather. My mother, who is a Latina, was abandoned by her biological mother, physically and emotionally abused in multiple relationships, and settled into a relationship with my stepfather when I was five years old. Together they have three children and three from other relationships.

I am the oldest of seven siblings and the only one of mixed races. I'm intentional about my identity as an Afro-Latina and passionate about experiencing both cultures simultaneously, although I will admit I am melanin challenged and lighter than most black women and I am not fluent in my native Spanish tongue. While I am supremely grateful to be biracial, this was not an easy journey, as I was often ostracized growing up because I did not meet other people's cultural expectations; *"You're not Black, you are red-boned - you don't know the struggle"*, or *"You're not a 'real' Latina if you don't speak Spanish."* I wasn't aware there were criteria for being "Black" or "Latina." These unfair expectations fused into my sense of self and belonging for a greater portion of my life than I should have allowed.

JACK OF ALL TRADES

I was raised in a traditional, strict, religious Hispanic/ Caribbean household. Growing up I was deeply influenced by the Arts *(music, dance, design, fine arts, etc.)*. As the oldest, my step- father had higher expectations for me to graduate and become independent. When I told him about my dreams of attending an art school he said *"Mija, you are a jack of all trades and a master of none."* This was because I could do a lot of things easily, but I never 'mastered' anything or fully committed to one thing.

Needless to say, I left home abruptly at 18 and joined the Air Force. At that age, I wasn't sure what he meant until I looked back over my professional career. I switched occupations every three years in the military until I separated after 10 years of service and in college, I changed my Bachelor's and Master's majors twice. In my mid-career, because of my status as a military wife, I left jobs every 3-4 years, however, I was fortunate to work in similar organizations, which required me to be a jack of all trades as a consultant and corporate trainer. I also worked in K-12 education and health & wellness, which required me to be adaptable and knowledgeable.

I traveled, climbed the career ladder, managed a healthy marriage and family, yet I was always feeling incomplete; there was a nagging notion deep inside that I was not enough. 90 days into a new executive role, I was feeling a bit exposed for my lack of executive-level experiences and began feeling offended and getting defensive about my expertise. I decided to invest in my personal and professional growth and hired an Executive Coach. I quickly realized that I was stuck in a loop and life was repacking and returning lessons to me that I was subconsciously avoiding. I was holding on to fears and coping with them, so I decided it was time to surrender and learn the lesson of receiving the blessing. My coach gave me homework to learn how to receive feedback from my relationships. The question was *"how are you experiencing me emotionally?"* Beyond the beautiful affirmations my friends and family shared about me, what was most enlightening was their honesty about my need to control or fix things and suppress my confidence or 'dim my light' for others' egos. Through this exercise of reflective listening, I realized, for most of my life, I've been trying to convince people I was relevant. Adding labels to my identity and adding layers to my expertise for others' validation and approval. Eventually I had to admit I was suffering from imposter syndrome because I never felt complete or whole & I never felt like I mastered anything. I would often over-explain who I was, trying to convince people that I am smart or important enough, yet in the back of my mind, I was worried they would discover that I'm not "qualified or experienced or fluent or cultured" enough for their standards. I was betraying myself by negotiating my own sense of integrity.

Who are we telling people that we are? Better yet, who are you *allowing* to tell you who you are? What is your origin story? My origin story started the day I was born, and it became clear to me that my journey was not over, and I needed to rewrite this narrative about who I was in the world. During a moment of meditation, I received a very loud and specific message - *forgiveness*! I was guided to create a spiritual journal dedicated to forgiving everyone by digging out the root cause of people's actions who have hurt, disappointed, discouraged, disrespected, and disposed of me emotionally, physically, and spiritually. The journal had to begin with me, then my parents and others.

I decided to release my fear of control and agreed to surrender to the journey; I opened my eyes to the life lessons unfolding before me, so I could align with my purpose. I needed to forgive myself for judging myself based on others' beliefs and expectations. I needed to forgive the man who violated my mother, accept the divine timing of my conception and release any judgment of his sins. I needed to forgive my mother for her unhealthy life choices and let go of the disappointment I felt when she did not fight back for herself. I needed to forgive my step-father for how he raised me with a fiery tongue and deemed me a "jack of all trades and a master of none," as if it were a curse, disappointment and failure. I now accept this as a blessing in disguise, because today I am adaptable, creative, and relatable. I also need to forgive everyone who consciously or unconsciously taught me I am not worthy of their time, energy, or attention. Today, I am choosing to vibrate higher, I forgive you and I release you!

HELLO, MY NAME IS "BEHATI"

In 2018, I was experiencing a strong universal calling to move in a new direction spiritually. Two years prior, I was on a quest to discover more about my cultural story and I desired a new identity that would align with both my ancestral DNA as an Afro-Latina with Indigenous roots, and my spiritual identity, unchained from the confines of the word religion. I chose the name **Behati,** which is a girl's name of African origin meaning *"blessed; she who brings happiness."* But I also loved the Urban Dictionary definition: *"a beautiful, exotic girl who is kick-ass and both mentally and physically strong."* Since then, I've been trying the name on for size, pronouncing and proclaiming it in new spaces and updating all my social media accounts; I'm even planning an official name change.

Near the end of 2019, I was in a fluid spiritual space of awareness and discovery, loving my new-ish identity, and I was excited about new revelations for my passions, and my purpose. I also began experiencing a disconnect from my workplace because my vision and personal values were not aligned. So, I took a leap of faith in the middle of a pandemic and economic uncertainty and walked away from that role. I was immediately blessed with a new position that also came with a huge promotion.

I was excited to be in a new role that I believed would allow my gifts and talents to match the organizational culture. Almost immediately, I began facing a new set of professional and personal challenges. Remember, previously I stated, *"life was repacking and returning lessons to me that I was subconsciously avoiding?"* In this case, I was, yet again, being challenged because my purpose was out of alignment with this new career experience. While I was seeing an Executive Coach, I had also recently decided that I wanted to become a Spiritual/Life Coach. I understood my challenges were reflecting areas where I was stuck in my own beliefs, but they were also necessary for me to experience, so I could effectively coach others. Once I accepted this revelation the lessons became clearer, more frequent, and becoming easier to overcome emotionally and spiritually.

One of my core strengths is connectedness and my value is serving others. My heart is filled with great joy when I can share my spiritual and artistic gifts and talents to impact others. So, I set out to volunteer in spaces to serve and empower youth around the Arts. Dancing has been a therapeutic talent I love to share with others. My friend says, *"when you're in your flow space that is your purpose and the universe will rise to meet you."* My heart desired to operate purposefully, so I became intentional about creating these experiences where I was in service to others.

ON PURPOSE

One day, I received a call from an acquaintance with whom I had worked on community projects. They excitedly propositioned me with a new executive position that would place me in areas that aligned closely with my purpose. I was speechless, humbled, and conflicted because I had only been in my new position for four months and was also in the middle of professional growth through Executive coaching. To be honest, self-judgment crept right back up, *"do I have the knowledge and emotional intelligence to lead others at this level for this new organization?"*

Like Dr. Strange in *Avengers: Infinity Wars*, I examined every possible personal outcome, as to why I should not explore this opportunity; I accepted the revelation that my reputation and character were valued in spaces where I wasn't even present, and I surrendered to be open and curious. I welcomed the opportunity to interview and I am now waiting at the stop sign of life for a sign from above to tell me which direction to take. Whatever the outcome, I am grateful for this universal validation that I am more than enough.

During a recent morning meditation, I received the most profound message about my purpose thus far: *You came into this life with a spiritual curriculum. Your soul agreed, before choosing to be born, to learn the lessons of the curriculum. Your spiritual curriculum has one aim; to get you back to God, truth, and your divine identity. So, trust that whatever and whoever shows up in your life, it's just a lesson designed to facilitate your journey back home.*

This is a passage from Iyanla Vanzant's Awakenings, which poetically describes the story of my journey home to my higher self. I no longer subscribe to coincidences. The past few years of my spiritual awakening have proven to me my life's journey to purpose has been divinely designed. I believe if you have life, you have purpose. The moment I was born was on purpose. The challenges and blessings of my life have been and will continue to be, on purpose. I am spiritually aware that I have the will to choose to live each experience, from this day forward, on purpose.

What do you know for sure?

All things work together for my own good - it's part of our soul's curriculum.

REFLECTION QUESTIONS

1. Who are you telling people you are?

2. Where are you holding unforgiveness?

3. How would you define your purpose?

BIOGRAPHY

Designer, Consultant, Mentor, and Positive Vibe Collaborator, Behati Hart is motivated by futuristic thinking and human-centered design. Behati is truly a jack of all trades with a career that spans over two decades, continents and industries while serving in the US Air Force, public service, and social innovation.

Behati's down-to-earth humor compels audiences to laugh while they learn, which is why she is consistently recognized and awarded for her motivational training, key-note presentations, and event experiences. She holds a Master of Arts in Human Behavior and is an aspiring spiritual and life coach. As a native of Chicago, Illinois, Behati embraces her multi-ethnic roots and uses her superpowers to energize youth and women empowerment programs.

"I'm not one to shy away from a dance battle or turn down free food" - Behati shares her playful and grateful heart with her two talented daughters, three funny dogs, and her life partner and fellow Air Force veteran, Kevin Hart (not-the-comedian).

BA in Business Administration.

She has earned several recognitions and awards as professional and entrepreneur.

Behati Hart
Email: betty.hart4@gmail.com
LinkedIn - linkedin.com/in/bettyhart

Yoly Magaña-Valencia

*"Success is not about how much money you make, it is about the
difference you make in people's lives."*

My mother, Lilia, was orphaned at the age of 10. Her
mother suffered from pneumonia shortly after giving birth to
the youngest of her siblings. She battled the disease for months
before she lost all chances. She died leaving my mother (who was
the second oldest of eight) to fend for herself and her siblings.
She had to look after herself and all her siblings, including an
eight-month-old baby. Lilia's father was consumed by alcohol
as he tried to cope with his wife's death. He just disappeared,
leaving his children all by themselves. As an orphan, it was not
easy for my mother to try to survive along with her siblings. She
used to say she wished she had had someone's help—I think that
is the reason she had such a gentle and humble heart always ready
to lend a hand or give advice.

My mother came to the US from a small rural village in
Michoacán, Mexico, when she was fourteen years old. Her
older brother arranged for her to be brought over to the US to
stay with her maternal grandmother in pursue of a better life.

Unfortunately, her grandmother was very tough with her and had her do all the house chores. It was a mystery for us why she was so upset and not happy at all to have her grandchild at home.

Mom got married to my father in Chicago, Illinois, at the age of 16. He comes from the same town in Mexico, but they met in Chicago. Like most women of her time, she was a housemaid, stayed home raising her children in the neighborhood of Pilsen, Chicago. Pilsen has always been a gateway for immigrants. We were all born and raised in Chicago.

My parents were overly strict and trusted nobody. This has to do with the fact they were immigrants in a country that did not feel like home—maybe worsen by all the hard circumstances my mom had to face as a child.

In my family, I was the only girl out of five. We totaled six, but my little sister was born well after I left home. As a girl I had to clean, cook—I was nearly seven when I learned my first recipes— and help with my younger siblings. There was no such idea of women empowerment because machismo was the rule; the ideology was that of the superiority and dominance of men over women. So, my brothers were encouraged to go to school and to pursue higher education, while I was told that only way to get out of home would be with a husband. I tried to challenge those stereotypes and prove anything my brothers could do, I would do it not only right but better.

When I was in high school, I joined the marching band and ROTC—my pressure valve from home. Even this was not easy. Both, my band teacher and my ROTC Sergeant, on different occasions, went to see my parents to request permission so that I could be in the band considering that would require some time after school. I dared tell them the truth that mom and dad were very strict and that I was expected to come home straight after school, which did not allow me that extra time for school practice.

I grew up to see my brothers doing lots of things that were forbidden to me, like hanging out with friends, riding a bike, playing outdoors. I realized the marginalization I was living through with time. This might have to do with old wounds my parents had not healed. They truly believed they were protecting me and that was the only possible way for them. Besides, my parents were all alone to raise their children, with no *abuelos* or other relatives to help. I like to think *abuelitos* would have made a difference in my life.

FIRST CAME LOVE

I met my husband in high school—we dated in my junior and senior years, though not sure if I should call it dating. Since I had no permission to go out, my boyfriend used to come over to have long conversations with me outside my house until my parents would have me get in. He kept visiting me like this for two years. While my class was busy with graduation preparations, I was planning my wedding because I was already engaged.

I was awarded a scholarship to UIC through the ROTC program. I loved school not only because it would get me out of my house, but because I enjoyed learning and always did well.

My parents were not fond of the idea, especially because it would require me to stay active in the ROTC program being the only girl—plus that was no place for a girl, as they saw it. And since the only way to leave my parents' home was with a husband, I got married two weeks after my high school graduation. I was already pregnant.

I was truly convinced I could do great if I studied. Shortly after giving birth to my daughter, I went back to school to get my associate degree in paralegal studies. That was my key to Corporate America.

I got my first job at the Leo Burnett advertising agency as administrative assistant for the Hispanic division. At first, I was excited about working with a bunch of Latinos with whom I thought would share similar experiences, but that was not the case. I still felt I did not belong and that I was not exploring my full potential. Then, I joined PR21, a public relations firm of The Edelman Company. I liked it too, but again it was not the place where I could accomplish big things.

I have been working for a year and a few months at PR21 when the 9/11 attacks took place in NYC. The September 11 attacks had an immediate negative impact on the US economy leading to the so called 2001 economic recession that resulted in rising unemployment. PR21 did not escape those circumstances and had to dismiss about 90% of the workforce to later cease business.

I had been looking for a job nearly for a year when I finally was referred for a position in the financial industry. I was hired as trust administrator for the Harris Bank—currently BMO—helping the bank's trust counsel with the handling of trusts. That was my first job in the financial area, and I learned a lot. I continued to feel not totally satisfied, though. So, I decided to get a real estate agent license and become a part-time licensed residential realtor. I just kept on increasing my financial knowledge. Meanwhile, my son was born. I quickly learned to manage my job, my part-time commitments, and motherhood. My career as realtor was short-lived because soon after came the housing market crash and I could not afford to pay the license fees. It was a very hard decision to make as I enjoyed being part of the real estate industry, but it was a reasonable decision to make for the sake of my family—now I was the mom of two!

Letting go of my real estate license pushed me to seek out other opportunities at BMO. BMO was the first organization where I saw employees being encouraged to grow and try new things. I was hired as office manager for the Corporate Finance Department of the bank. I was always open to all the new opportunities, and grateful. Within a few weeks I had taken on this new position, I found out I was expecting my third baby. I wondered how they would react to this as they knew I had a toddler at home. I had already been on maternity leave once before while working at the bank so I was worried this could affect my new position. Thus, I was never absent despite of being sick—I even hid behind my desk to vomit into my trash can. I tried not to tell the manager and the board about my pregnancy until it was physically obvious.

After my third child was born, every time I needed to talk to my manager she would make some comment like: "Let me guess, you are pregnant again." I realized I was right about feeling my position was at risk for being a working mom.

I had a strong work ethic and was very loyal as most Latinos. I fulfilled my duties with my best efforts. I always kept my head down and never took part in activities of the organization outside my job. I would go to the office, do my work, and then go home. My number one priority was my three children.

One day, one of the very few Latinos in the department and the organization named Ramiro J. Atristain-Carrion invited me to join him to participate in an event as volunteer. Ramiro was Vice President in the finance group and was very active in the organization. He promoted the creation of a Hispanic Networking Group within the organization to foster a network for professional development among Latino employees. The Hispanic Networking Group would later have an official board. This was my first involvement with the Latinos community within the bank. In the event hosted at BMO, I was at the welcome desk registering guests after office hours. For the first time in my life, I was experiencing satisfaction and fulfillment as I was doing something else that exceeded my regular 9-5.

My involvement with the Bank continued to grow. Ramiro always seemed to be particularly interested in my work and I informally considered him my mentor. He persuaded me to go back to school to finish my undergraduate degree. While completing my studies, he became my advisor and always advocated for me. The Hispanic Networking Group later turned into the BMO's Latino Alliance. By recommendation of Ramiro, I was appointed Treasurer. That was my first time serving on a board. Being a part of a board with other Latinos really changed my perspective but also educated me on Corporate America and how underrepresented Latinos are. I was progressively more committed to the community and I felt an obligation towards my peers. The fact of being an active member of the organization and the Latino community opened up many doors for me, including other positions I could have never even considered if I had remained in doubt about my skills, talents, and accomplishments. I managed to get back into the real estate industry and go back to school to get my MBA.

I am a proud first-generation Latina that struggled through life and had a very non-traditional journey. I have learned from experience that it was not until I started being unselfish, giving back to the community, and helping other fellow Latinos that my career took off. As I reflect, it was not only my hunger for knowledge and growth that helped me move forward, embrace the change, and succeed, it took another empowered individual to tap me on the shoulder and take it upon himself to empower me. My passion to help others is based on my own experience through which I have learned that once you feel empowered, you have the responsibility to empower others.

REFLECTION QUESTIONS

1. Have you experienced perseverance in life?

2. How important is it to you to give back to your community?

3. How do you empower others?

BIOGRAPHY

Yoly Magaña-Valencia is currently a Senior Consultant in Workplace Strategy Consulting at JLL, a Global Real Estate and Investment Management firm headquartered in Chicago. She currently serves as Engagement Officer for Casa Central's Emerging Leaders Auxiliary Board.

Yoly has received several recognitions for her work in the Community. These include a recognition by Negocios Now: Who's who in Hispanic Chicago, a Workforce Impact award by Prospanica, and several recognitions for her commitment and leadership as Director of Education for Prospanica's Summer Enrichment Program.

She is excited to lead work that emphasizes on education and social service to improve underserved and underrepresented communities in Chicago. She is on a mission to change the narrative among Latinas and Wealth. She is the founder of Latinas Who Trade. Latinas Who Trade was created to provide education and resources to Latinas in our community who are interested in learning about investing and trading.

On a personal note, Yoly is a Certified Yoga Teacher (born and raised in Chicago) that subscribes to the idea that giving ourselves to our communities is essential in our development and ability to reach our potential with both leadership and personal success. Yoly is passionate about making a difference and is a leader who inspires not only through words but through actions

Yoly graduated with honors from DePaul University with an MBA in Real Estate, Finance and Investment and a BA in Business Administration. She is still married to her husband of almost 25 years with two daughters and a son, who are her everyday inspiration to do good.

Yoly Magaña-Valencia
latinaswhotrade@gmail.com
(773) 398-8994

Wanda Malone

"Live your Life to the Fullest. The sky's the limit!"

I was born in Cambridge, Massachusetts and moved to Puerto Rico at 9. Growing up in Puerto Rico was not the easiest and was a big adjustment for our family. My mom was resilient and taught us to never give up. I always knew I would be a strong-minded person growing up with such a powerful and strong mother as a role model.

I always wanted to attend college in the US- one of them being University of Wisconsin-Madison. I remember the entire experience as if it were yesterday. The principal from my high school came to our social studies class and asked to speak to me. So, I walked into his office and he handed me a letter. I had applied to a number of universities and had letters sent to my high school, as I did not want to disappoint my mother for applying to schools far away. I opened the letter, read only a couple lines and it hit me.

It sank in quickly; I had just been accepted to University of Wisconsin-Madison. I could not believe my eyes, as this would soon become a huge transition for my family and me, but one I knew I had to embrace. I wanted to ensure that I graduated from a top university and gave myself every opportunity to follow my dreams. I did. I told my mom, and although she was devastated to see me leave, she knew this would be such an amazing experience and opportunity. In August of 1987, I left Puerto Rico to pursue my dreams and a better life.

MY NEW JOURNEY BEGINS ABRUPTLY

The years at UW Madison were not easy: learning English, adjusting to the weather, being one of over 46K students, and navigating the campus were all overwhelming. I never let this bring me down; I was determined to do this for the betterment of myself and my family. I would call my mom crying because I missed my family. It was tough as hell, but I was determined to graduate, since this would be the path for a great future. I was a first-generation college graduate. It was a difficult feat, but one that I am very proud of; I earned my degree!

MY NEW LIFE TAKES SHAPE

During my college years, I met my husband and we dated for a long time. We married in August 2002. I told him that I would not have kids until after I enjoyed traveling and experiencing life; then we would marry and have kids. This man has been my rock and my support through it all.

In 2003, our first son was born, and we were living life to its fullest...I cared for our son and decided that I would stay at home to raise him. Our son DJ met some milestones, but there were some red flags and mommy gut feelings that concerned me. I brought up my concerns to our pediatrician and she said boys talk later, to not stress, not believe everything I read... At 18 months, we sought an Early Intervention Evaluation and he qualified for services; he was diagnosed with Autism at 2 ½.

YOU'RE NEVER PREPARED FOR NEWS LIKE THIS

The developmental pediatrician told us our son would never be conversational and we should consider putting him in an institution. She told us to have him re-evaluated again in 6 months. Hearing this was like someone killed my soul and I cried for years. I fell into severe depression, and never told our family about this dreadful diagnosis. For about a year and a half we kept the diagnosis to ourselves; not because of shame or fear, but because we needed to grieve and go through the emotions. We knew something was not right, but hearing these words was devastating. We had so many dreams for our first-born son and didn't know what was next; it truly felt like a death.

I researched online to educate and empower myself with as much information as I could. It was then I decided I would not let this take me down any further... I realized I needed to do *everything* within my power to help our son. I searched at all hours into the night and stayed awake until late hours searching and learning more about Autism. One day, I decided I could either keep mourning or take the bull by its horns and move it forward. I have always been a determined person, and nothing was going to stop me from trying to find ways to help our son... and that is what I did.

DJ has gone through a lot, as many special-needs kids have, but he has gained skills every step of the way! We did everything, including: ABA therapy, diet change, chelation, HBOT, alternative medicine, neurofeedback, speech, occupational therapy, and so much more. I was determined to try anything noninvasive.

All that determination and resilience is what helped me ensure our son had the resources and support he needed... my son's journey has become my driving force, my determination and motivation to do what I do now; *our son DJ is my "why!"* He taught me what it is to be fragile, strong, emotional, and reckless, but most importantly, to never give up hope. The sky's the limit!

HOPE SPRINGS ETERNAL

When DJ was 15 months old our second son was born. Jayden was the happiest, and most curious, determined kid. He learned quickly that we did not live a "normal" family life. We went from therapies to therapies; at times we could not go places, parties or dinners. Jayden was what we called our built-in therapist- he always looked out for his brother and ensured to help him at every step of the way. We taught Jayden life is not easy, but that in our family, we always smile, laugh, cry, and *never* give up! Jayden has grown up to be such a passionate young man. Living the life of a special needs sibling is not easy. Many times, he is embarrassed, and I am sure wondering why, but he has always taken the approach that we stick together as a family no matter what is thrown our way. I know it has not been an easy journey for Jayden, but I cannot wait to see what the future holds for him.

INCLUSION FOR ALL

Both of our boys have food allergies and our youngest son always asked me why he couldn't have Goldfish, or Cheez-It snacks like other kids. This was a turning point for me. I approached our school district's Food and Allergy Committee with a full plan to do sample testing, find volunteers, and have food donated for us to create an inclusion opportunity for our sons. In 2009, District 204 was the first in Illinois to offer a full gluten-free menu. When I created this program, I wanted it to mirror the regular menu; if another student had the choice of pizza or nuggets, then our kids and others in the district would have the same gluten/casein-free option. I am proud to say that this program still exists in District 204.

THE FIGHTER WITHIN ME FIGHTS FOR A CAUSE

I knew I needed to create a platform for resources and network opportunities for special-needs families in our communities. This is when, Autism Family Foundation (AFF) was formed. AFF is a not-for-profit, small, local organization that helps special-needs families. We have hosted an Annual Special-Needs Holiday Event for the last eight years; this is an event the community looks forward to attending, where they can connect with other special-needs parents and not feel judged.

Through the years, I have helped so many families navigate the overwhelming process of the IEP/504 and help them find resources. After working in corporate America for years, I decided to help our special-needs family's full time. I ventured to start my own business and followed my mission...my higher calling was to serve and help our special-needs families.

I have been a bilingual, English and Spanish IEP Coach/ Educational Advocate for over 13 years, where I guide and teach people the ins and outs of the IEP process; I stand by their side, ensuring the students obtain the support and services they need, while preparing them for the future. I take a collaborative approach when working with schools. I have found that this approach makes meetings run a bit smoother and the districts appreciate my work. My intent is to ensure that every special-needs family understands, knows their options, and can advocate for their kids with knowledge and the proper resources. This is how Wanda Malone Educational Services was formed. My company exists solely to provide resources, and guide and empower families to navigate the overwhelming IEP/504 process within the schools nationwide.

I pride myself on being able to think outside of the box and create inclusion opportunities when they do not exist. I never take no for an answer and believe if there is a will, there is *always* a way!

IT ALL MAKES SENSE NOW

Another big mission of mine in 2020, was to help and support underserved, special-needs families by obtaining grants to help families that are not able to afford the services. Then COVID came along. 2021/2022 is the year to make this happen; this is my mission and calling!

In 2021, I created the IEP Inner Circle (English & Spanish)- an online training that special-needs parents can do at their own pace; they have lifetime access to over 12 videos, checklists, private Facebook group and so much more. This was my interim plan to help as many families during COVID.

Life has certainly thrown me many curve balls, but this has never stopped me from pushing through barriers even during the most difficult and challenging times. Often, I'd say to myself *"I'm done,"* but then I'd look at my WHY and continue.

IF YOU CAN CONCEIVE IT, YOU CAN ACHIEVE IT

Being a first-generation college graduate meant the world to me, but now I have ingrained in my kids how important education is and that regardless of what you do in life once you earn a degree the sky is truly the limit. Being a Hispanic woman, I always had to prove myself in corporate America. The majority of my corporate career was in Human Resources, managing employees and multiple facilities including international facilities. Often, I sat in meetings with executives and, being a young Hispanic woman, I always had to go the extra mile to earn respect and collaboration with the other executives. This taught me to never allow anyone to talk down to me or make me feel less. On the contrary, I have never been afraid to speak up. Eventually, I was considered an equal member of the executive team.

Starting Wanda Malone Educational Services has been such a blessing. I love helping special-needs families. Thanks to my Spanish, my name has been shared throughout the community and nationwide. I am so passionate about what I do, and I want to ensure that every single family I help is guided through this process and also learns along the way. As a special-needs mom and IEP Coach/Advocate, I am able to take out any and all emotions while we are attending our meetings. This is a huge component of creating successful meetings.

PATIENCE AND TEMPO MATTER

Everything I do in life now comes from helping people, uplifting culture and most importantly my heritage. I will always ensure my family and others around me know where I came from, who I am and how all my experiences have made me who I am today. I am a strong, passionate, devoted, professional, and a determined Hispanic woman that is here to support other families in our community.

REFLECTION QUESTIONS

1. What would you do if you received an unexpected medical diagnosis for your child that would change how you envisioned their future? How would you cope?

2. What is your "why" and how do you stay focused?

3. Which of the lessons you learned in my story do you see applying to your life and why?

BIOGRAPHY

Wanda Malone is a special-needs mom and Bilingual IEP Coach/Advocate. She has been an advocate in the special-needs' community for over 13 years. Her role as an IEP Coach is to guide, assist and create powerful/meaningful IEP that is student centered, and ensuring that our kids are prepared for the future. Her collaborative approach equals success for the students. She helps special-needs families and the entire IEP team navigate the IEP journey with a plan, creating functional goals and preparing the child for the future!

If you want to learn more about IEPs and learn how to apply these options, Join the IEP Inner Circle. This is an online, self-paced training with weekly live Q&As.

Areas of Expertise:
- Autism, ADHD, Executive Functioning, Dyslexia, Dysgraphia, Dyscalculia and P.A.N.S/P.A.N.D.A.S.

Affiliations and Training:
- Member of National Organization for Special Education Attorneys and Advocate since 2017
- Wright's Law Training
- Executive Functioning & Social Thinking Training
- 3,700+ hours in IEP Training, Advocacy, Goal Writing, Resolution and Conflict Management, Strength- Based IEP
- Advanced Advocacy Training through the National Organization of Special Ed Attorneys and Advocates 2021
- Board Member of the Aurora Advisory Commission on Disabilities. Appointed in December 2020 by the City of Aurora Mayor and Council
- State of Illinois Approved Trainer for IEP's

Wanda Malone

www.wandamaloneeducationalservices.com

Facebook Wanda Malone Educational Services

Instagram@ Wanda Malone Educational Services

wanda@wandamaloneeducationalservices.com

THE UNEXPECTED

Olga Medina

"Life is not measured by the number of breaths we take,
but by the moments that take our breath away."
—Maya Angelou

The first time someone told me that I should write my story, I felt bewildered and laughed. I asked myself: who would be interested in knowing about me? Many people told me I was successful, but that made me feel uncomfortable; I was the only one who could not appreciate my true worth. I came to realize the importance of self-love and self-confidence; I know that there are many Olgas out there that, just like me, find it hard to believe in themselves... It is important that you have faith in yourself; you just have to make the decision and wait for the unexpected.

Waiting for the unexpected entails doing things though not expecting something in return; this means that if you work with love, dedication and responsibility in every aspect of your life, you may be rewarded for your work, but sometimes that gratification is even greater when it comes from inside yourself and that is when the unexpected may arrive: you may be promoted to a better position, you may become your own boss, or you may run your own business or even become an entrepreneur.

Never stop learning, get in touch with people who inspire you, read books that reach your heart, do what you love, do it without expecting anything in return, live your life and each day as if it were the last. Without knowing it, I have been doing all that since the day I dared follow my heart. I made things happen... I know what I want. I pushed myself to act. I now take more risks. I make fewer mistakes. I anticipate problems. I accept the truth. I see the big picture. I deal with one thing at a time.

BUSINESS LESSONS

I grew up in a solid family; my father was a musician and my mother a merchant. I come from a very large family of nine. My parents were my role model, I have always admired them deeply; they come from Ocotlan Puebla Chila de la Sal, a town where chickens and donkeys woke everyone up in the mornings. My father always loved music and he learned to play the guitar and the trumpet at the age of 11 thanks to a small old radio my grandfather had at the time. He was only 15 years old when he asked for my then 14-year-old mother's hand. Those times were definitely different. After marriage, they moved to Mexico City where opportunities made it possible to offer us a better future as the soil was exhausted in their hometown.

Over time, my father formed a band with some other musicians and did very well in terms of money. He was a very smart man. When I was a child, he taught me how to multiply; then I learnt that he had only completed up to second grade and that made me admire him even more. As a 10-year old girl, I used to witness that my father gave money to my mother to administer for the expenses of the house. So, I started doing the same by saving half of my allowance; I think that was my beginning as an entrepreneur.

In the winter of 1993, I met Evelia—a friend and business partner. Just about three months before graduation as stylists, Evelia and I launched our first business together called "OLGA EVELIA BEAUTY SALON." Oh, God, I really had no idea of running any business! I was only 17 and merely following my dreams. In 1994, I met Juan, the love of my life. With the support of Evelia, Juan, and my family, we managed to surf the wave. I learnt a lot from that first business experience (to have a partner, to deal with customers, how to communicate), and all that was very much useful to pave my way to build what it would be my own company.

Three months after I graduated and while operating the salon, in 1995, I married Juan, who worked as a farmer and as a truck driver. I soon got pregnant. Living in Mexico was turning harder each day. And, so, we decided to move to the US. A huge change of place, people, weather, and language! We were very young to see the risky move we were making. We just had in mind to provide a better future to our family.

EMBRACE RESPONSIBILITY, NOT BLAME

On June 20, 1995, the adventure began. I was seven months pregnant when we took a bus to the city of Tijuana, where we were expected to be taken to the US border. Juan and I got separated, and we were told that I would be taken by plane or car; he had to go first while I stayed in Tijuana with my godfather and his daughter for six weeks before we could cross the border. It was summer and the weather was really hot. We were approached by migration officers on three occasions, I was desperate as I had had no news from Juan. We stayed four days on the hills drinking water only as we had eaten the only bread we had very soon. We crossed on fours with elbows and knees; it was really difficult for me with my eight-month's pregnancy, as my belly was almost touching the floor. When I got to San Diego, the woman who welcomed me looked at me and said: "how come you got here like this, girl?" She stared at me and started crying, I did not know what was happening! I took a bath and while the water washed away the mud and blood from my body, elbows and knees, I embraced myself and my belly, and I started crying; I realized that I could have died or, even worse, lost my baby.

But that was not even all. From San Diego we had to cross the border at San Clemente, where we laid in the trunk of a car. After several hours, our bodies were numb; we reached California and headed to an empty apartment where we were locked up for a week, without food, only water, and sleeping on the floor. I still had no news from Juan, I was very sad, and I could only pray for him to be ok. "It's time," the *coyote* said. "You're going to New York!"

I would finally reunite with my husband; he and my sister would be waiting for me in New Jersey. I will never forget the day I finally got to New York, or when I got on the plane, or the face of my husband when we finally had that never-ending hug. We cried, kissed, and he promised we would never separate or go through any of that again until we could get our residence.

On August 4, 1995, I got to NJ and on October 17, 1995, my beautiful boy Adrián was born; he has always been my blessing and the energy that kept me going. My life changed completely in only one year. I had become a wife and a mother at a very early age, moved to a foreign country where I could not speak the language, and decided that my career as a cosmetologist had to be put on hold. No regrets. Then, in 1999, I was blessed again giving birth to Rose, my sweet life treasure.

THE GOAL THAT DRIVES YOU

Adrián started first grade and the first days at school were really hard for him as we only spoke Spanish at home. After a few months, the teacher called us to have a meeting. I had to go alone since my husband worked 24/7 at that time. I could not understand a word and Adrián had to translate everything the teacher said. I was surprised to see how much he had learnt in only a few months. I felt embarrassed that my 6-year old child was officiating as interpreter. Then, we lived in Fairlawn NJ, where most people were Russians, Italians, and Jews. I did not speak a word in English, so I decided to go to school and get my GED to be able to help my two children.

I came back to work in 2000. For 7 years, I worked at a salon called Pamper, a lounge where only English was spoken so I learnt a lot, and that helped me communicate. Many things happened during that time. In 2006, we finally got our legal residences and were able to go back to Mexico after 11 years. In 2009, I began to study to get my NJ cosmetologist license. I cannot tell it was easy. My days started at 6 in the morning and I used to go to bed at 1 AM—which caused me stress and alopecia. I decided to work partially from home to be more available for my children. My life lesson from that: keep a humble heart and embrace people from all walks of life.

MY COMPANY, MY RESPONSIBILITY

Doing my best and with the help of my family, I continued educating myself in every aspect of life. Life put me great mentors on the way and each of them made a difference in my life. I took many managerial courses to get ready. The more I knew about how to get my business started, the more afraid I was, but at the same time I felt the rush of adrenaline that kept me moving.

Finally, on May 16, 2015, SIMPLY YOU HAIR STUDIO AND SPA opened its doors. It is curious how life works; I am at exactly the same place where I started working as an employee, but now I am its owner. Since then, the path was full of blessings and challenges; much has happened in my personal and professional life, also my health: several surgeries, including kidney, appendix, and gallbladder, ovarian cancer. It has not been easy, there are still days when I feel I would rather stay in bed. In the end, when I look around I realize it is not a question of money, but of how much personal growth I have achieved. I feel blessed, powerful, proud, and I have the most precious treasure to support me: MY FAMILY.

My husband and my children are also entrepreneurs. Since 2018, Gaby's Pizza & Grill is open for business. Adrián is a partner at the restaurant and manages his own printing business—A Sharper Image. Rose helps as receptionist at the salon and as cashier at the pizza place, while maintaining great enthusiasm at attending school.

I went from not knowing what to do with my life to finding a job that turned into my career, and ultimately my career turned into my vision. People frequently ask me if having my own salon is my American dream and I usually say "no." I am a visionary and having my own salon is only part of the dream.

The past, the adversity, the decisions we make, our mistakes and experiences involve change; they are part of life and all that led me to where I stand today, to whom I am now. Better things are yet to come, and I am ready to share all that with my family, friends, and the whole world!

REFLECTION QUESTIONS

1. What is the unexpected to you?

2. Who are those around you? Do they support you?

3. What part of my story had the greatest impact on you?

BIOGRAPHY

Olga Medina is the founder of Simply You Hair Studio—a women and minority-owned business in Bergen County. As a native of Mexico with 25 years of experience working in salons in the US, she has always wanted to help people look and feel their best and express themselves in their own unique way. The salon she runs specializes in hair color, trends, and cuts.

The three words that best define Olga are: "passionate," "caring," and "creative." One of the things that truly inspire Olga's creativity is clients. As a woman with straight hair who is passionate about curls, Olga has pushed herself to find a way to help her "curly hair community."

Years of concentrated work have led her to develop the ultimate curly haircut. The Simply You Curly Cut enhances your curls according to the frame provided by your face shape, hair texture, and favorite trends to give you the style of your dreams.

Currently, Olga's entire team is trained in this specialized skill, as well as in what she calls the "Simply You Technique." The staff focuses on creating dimensional coloring and personalized cuts while maintaining healthy hair and enhancing each customer's natural beauty and diversity. Come and visit the salon and enjoy being Simply You!

Olga Medina
Email: info@simplyyouhairspa.com
Facebook: simplyyouhairstudio
Instagram: @Curlycutsbyolga
Instagram: @simplyyouhairstudio
Google: Simply You Hair Studio & Spa LLC
Slogan: Be the best version of yourself, be simply you!

Monica Morales

"Never let a broken heart define your destiny"

One day a lady looked at me and said: "I can see that you hate failure." Those words from a stranger made me realize that such a statement was absolutely true. At that moment, I was going through a separation after 20 years of marriage and my heart was broken into a thousand pieces. My choices were either to seek counseling, to take depression pills, or to start a real estate business. I went with option number three.

May 2018 was the date for the opening of Extreme Realty-Elmwood Park and I was ready to begin this new chapter in my life. I remember one special friend who truly trusted and followed me blindly saying "You got this." And she was right. In less than two years, I had become the proud owner of three real estate offices. Yes! THREE!

LIFE LESSONS

I was lucky enough to have the most wonderful parents as I grew up. However, since they had to work so much, my sisters and I were left to fend for ourselves. Unfortunately, at the age of 15, I got involved in a relationship with a highly manipulative man—in fact, I did not know any better—and I ran away from home. Many people have no idea about this episode of my life, including my children. But then I realized my story can help other young girls in the same situation and so they could see hope. No man should be allowed to intimidate us. I really hurt my parents with my actions. That is possibly why I have been so overprotective with my children. I have tried to teach them good values and principles and to defend themselves so they would not fall into the same trap I did. Thank God, I had the chance to apologize to my parents for my mistakes. Now I know they are proud of me and that is the best reward I can treasure from them. My parents never gave up on me and decided to send me to Guatemala. It was quite hard for me because I barely spoke Spanish—much less read and/or wrote in that language. Quite a huge challenge to start my life all over at the age of 15.

I was in a foreign country where the native language was Spanish, and I had no choice but to learn it. I did my best to get skilled. Not long after living there, I was able to have a full-blown conversation in Spanish.

Was I upset I had to live with my *Abuelita* for a while at first? Certainly! But now I am eternally thankful to my parents for that move. And, *Abuelita: Gracias por todo lo que hizo por mí.* *Abuelita* would keep an eye on me like a hawk. I used to think she was a little OCD (obsessive compulsive disorder), but I appreciate all the things I learned with her. I remember she would rub my head every night until I fell asleep. This lasted for a few years, then my parents decided to leave Chicago and start a new life in Guatemala. Another huge move for my family, but I had two other sisters that needed to be raised in a safer environment. My sisters and I—as I said before—grasped this opportunity to learn about life. We would be entirely different persons if not for that tremendous change. I stayed in Guatemala for six years before I came back to Chicago at age 21 for a new adventure.

HEARTBROKEN

When my marriage ended, I remember crying myself to sleep for months. Until today, many people still do not know I am separated. I felt embarrassed to be single after so many years of marriage. I planned my whole life, though this was not on the agenda. How could I tell my friends that I was no longer married? I was devastated. However, such pain drove my inner power to turn me into a stronger woman.

One day I said to myself: *"Enough. It is time to take control of my life."* No more asking myself how was I wrong? It takes two to tango and we were both equally responsible for the failure of our relationship. It was definitely not going to be the end of the world.

In July 2019, Extreme Realty-Cicero followed by Extreme Realty-Midway in November 2019 came into operation. Two new offices in the same year. What was I thinking? Was I crazy? In less than two years I have launched three real estate agencies. Two wonderful people were my great supporters in this daunting adventure and helped me run the business. The three offices keep on growing.

So, do not let anyone say: Don't do it! This is my first-hand experience: I DID IT! Working hard has helped me not to fall into depression. Work was my way of coping with the fact that my marriage had ended. I was in great distress for a while, but the more it hurt, the harder I worked. And when I felt lost and did not have my love to share my success stories with, I prayed a lot to God, who always listens. He gave me that peace of mind and that almighty hug I was eager for.

Finally, we realized we were better off as friends. Together we raise our two healthy and amazing children Destiny and David Jr. We are extremely proud of both of them. All my efforts now are dedicated to them. My children are my motivation. I refuse to stick to the idea that I may fail at anything. Life is too short, and we all deserve to be happy; we cannot settle for less. As I sit here and write this, I am fighting COVID. I have come to realize that I have always been on the go. My greatest desire is for my business to be successful; at the same time, though, I really pursue to enjoy life. Today, I say emphatically to myself: it is time to let go of the past. I am no longer ashamed of my failed marriage. I have no regrets because otherwise I would not be the person I am today.

STAY POSITIVE

Ladies, we have to be prepared to be hurt, struggle, and sacrifice to make it happen. Some people may tell you that your dreams are impossible, that the challenge is too great, but as long as you believe in yourself, there are no limits. A good friend of mine pronounced the following words when giving a speech: "It is not how many times you fall, it is how many times you get up." I am standing tall and proud and I apologize for any mistakes I have made. There are no constraints to the capacity to learn and to grow and to do the best we can accomplish.

So, Ladies, you will see that even when you feel like it is the end of the world, you still have that amount of energy and the brave heart required to make it to the finish line. Just believe in yourself. Quitting is not an option. Once you find out what your purpose in this world is, you need to run towards it. No matter how hard the truth is, do not be afraid of taking on your challenges and making them happen. It is like a marathon in which you need to keep running without looking back because the sensation of achieving your goal is amazing.

If you ask me if I have ever cried in my circumstances? Definitely! Several times I cried because I felt sad, upset, frustrated, lost, and alone. I have cried with joy countless times because I am thankful to God for all the blessings he has shown me. I have learned that my sole and unique competitor is nobody but myself.

And when the time comes to celebrate a victory, do not hesitate to take pride and merit for all the hard work you have pledged, invested, and harvested. No other person is to get the credits but YOU. Happiness is something only you can manage and control. Be your own boss and get ready to plan the rest of your life journey so that it really happens.

Currently, I count with an amazing team of the greatest and

kindest agents devoted to help families make their dreams come true. I can describe the enormous satisfaction I feel with my business as the best feeling in the world. A special thanks to all my Extreme Agents for believing in me.

REFLECTION QUESTIONS

1. How do you show that you take responsibility for your life and tackle obstacles regardless of how hard they may seem?

2. Who sets the highest expectations for you? Are you living up to them?

3. What "business lessons" do you think I have learned? How would you put such a lesson into practice?

BIOGRAPHY

Monica Morales is a Chicago-born real estate entrepreneur who has been in the business since 1998. She has engaged in the huge project of helping families take their biggest financial and emotional decision in life. She acknowledges and honors clients' trust in her by carrying out her job with unmatched devotion: an outstanding quality that makes her stand out of her competitors. As a Managing Broker, her first priority is to make families happy. She pays thorough attention to their requirements and needs and works recklessly to come to a successful outcome in every transaction. She assures clients a home-buying process full of fun, easiness, and without stress. No matter the type of transaction, either an acquisition or a sale, she is completely available to clients at any time of the day to respond to any inquiries or when they need to express their concerns. She would love to help you through one of the toughest (and most gratifying) decisions you may take in your life. She is just a phone call away.

Monica Morales
Mobile: 773 406 1900
www.extremerealtyhomes.com

Cristina Nuñez

"Think more about your blessings than your burdens."

Growing up in a household where I would sometimes sleep with an ice pack to combat the heat when our electricity was cut off, I still never felt that I came from a home that was missing anything. My mother always kept my heart full even when her bank account wasn't. I was raised to know my worth comes from what I make of myself and how high I hold myself up to my values. I had to keep my head in the game, finish my degrees, be financially independent, and never depend on a man.

I never had ambitions of being a leader, yet here I am, the owner of a successful business that improves lives daily. I am living the American dream of going to college, getting a job in my field, and soon enough, becoming my own boss. Most importantly, I'm an inspiration because I am living the life my mother dreamed for me.

MIAMI LIVING - BEING LATINA

Being raised in Miami, the exposure to different accents, cultures, foods, and customs is astounding! Between the blend of cultures, languages, and tropical paradises where one can socially gather, I don't see myself ever leaving Miami for too long. Living and working in the downtown, financial district of Brickell, there is more diversity other than Spanish-speaking cultures and endless possibilities for building a community from all walks of life.

My parents met in English class in San Jose, California, after being pioneers in their families, moving from their respective countries of Ecuador and Nicaragua. My household was very Hispanic-American; I would speak Spanish with my *abuelitas,* but English with my parents and sister. Speaking English at home is something many Hispanic households see as a sin, *"then you'll lose your Spanish!"* —and lose my Spanish I did. As I grew up around American anglo kids, Jewish kids, and not many other Hispanic-Americans in my advanced and gifted classes, my *gringa* accent got stronger and stronger. In my tween years I would refuse to speak my broken Spanish outside of talks with my *abuelitas.* As I got older, *gracias a Dios,* I learned to truly appreciate the value of a second language and the ways we use this part of ourselves to build community and share culture. Thanks to my fiancé and his Cuban-Peruvian-Brazilian family, I could not escape practicing my Spanish and I now speak it fluently. Building my Spanish, I gained a whole new side to my Latina pride, family unity, and said *adios* to my *gringa* accent. Now I regularly speak Spanish in business, which allows me to give families access to resources and education in a language they can understand.

OWN IT AND SHOW UP

Sometimes in life, we get curveballs that put our path on a new trajectory. Once on this new path we need to decide what to do—own it and show up, or let opportunities pass us by. I often meet parents and families at a time where their life's latest curveball is either noticing their child needs specialized help in an area of development, is Neurodivergent, or has a diagnosis of a developmental difference such as Autism, speech delay, ADHD, Down Syndrome, or GDD. There is a vast difference in a child's life trajectory with parents that own it and show up to therapy, versus families that wait and hope for their child to catch up on their own. I am blessed to work with kids and adults who have so much love and light to reciprocate because we glow with them when we give them our undivided professional attention and love. For some parents, we give them a sigh of relief knowing they are not alone fighting this battle to help their child be the best version of themselves; they are showing up too. In practice, ABA is a comprehensive therapy aimed at improving skills across developmental domains like speech and social interaction skills. I organize a collaborative team approach with speech therapists, neurologists, occupational therapists, teachers, physical therapists, and parents across South Florida to make bigger community impacts.

I've come to run a six-figure earning business before the age of 30 because I kept showing up. The grind was real and gritty, working different jobs with different families from sunup to sundown. At one point I would show up at 8 AM to my teaching position, leave for an after-school ABA therapy job with siblings I would see back-to-back, then head home at 8 PM. I didn't feel burnout for a while, because I genuinely loved being the one impacting so many kids' progress through showing up and doing the work. Three years into that grind, I looked around and saw people with similar business structures, less experience, and much less passion for their job, and began to feel that I was meant for something more. Then one afternoon, leaving my full-time job as a teacher at a specialized Autism school, heading to my part time ABA therapy job, life threw me a curveball that set my life on a new trajectory.

It was an exceptionally rainy day in Miami, where it seemed the "on/off" setting of our rain was stuck in the "on" position. I lost control of my car when my car hydroplaned on the highway spinning across 3 lanes until I collided with the median wall, throwing my body out of the driver's seat toward the passenger seat window, facing oncoming traffic. My first *carro del año*, a new Honda Civic lease I could afford under my own name on a teacher's salary, was wrecked. As I came to realize what was happening, I felt an unbearable sharp pain in my right leg and feared the worst. I took a deep breath and looked at my toes that were visible since my flats flew off during the collision, then sighed with relief that my toes were moving—I was not paralyzed. My head did not hit the concrete median like my car because my leg hit the middle console, stopping my body from flying further headfirst into the median wall of the highway, but the impact ended up breaking my femur, the bone in my thigh-the biggest bone in the human body. Through surgery to put a metal rod with screws though my hip, leg, and knee, to living in the hospital through rehab and therapies and learning to walk again, God gave me the blessing in disguise of opening up my time, letting me realize my value and allowing me to set myself up to be my own boss. In a few years' time, I would rebuild the strength in my legs, but equally important, I built up the strength in my self-confidence and professional skills, to become an inspirational leader and business owner that owns it and shows up to get the job done.

THE FUTURE IS *LIMITLESS*

This car accident was my opportunity to do more with myself than be stuck in a teaching position with no room for growth. My car accident opened the door for me continue working with the special needs population I love, using the science that I love; I did not return to the teaching position after the car accident to pursue ABA therapy full time. I was halfway done with my Master's degree, which lit the fire in me to finish faster and stronger than ever. I was helping new kids say their first words, I was making more money, I had more flexibility in my schedule, and things were looking better than ever as I spread the magic of ABA therapy throughout Miami. I was with a client at summer camp at the JCC Miami Beach during yoga class, when I received an unexpected call from my mom. I ensured the client was with a safe adult and took the phone call by the door. She told me bravely, holding back tears, the doctors found a mass on one of her breasts that had been leaking a discharge and these were symptoms of breast cancer. For the first time ever, I broke down crying in front of a room full of people.

The following few months involved me being my mom's support system and backbone at all her appointments across town. I knew again then to think more about my blessings than my burdens. God works in mysterious ways. As a schoolteacher, there was no way I would have had the flexibility to be taking days off every week to be with my mom through her doctor's appointments, surgeries, chemotherapy, and radiation appointments. We got through her treatments as I got through my last semesters of my online master's degree. 2018 turned out to be a year of incredible celebrations. We celebrated my mom's last days of chemo and radiation therapy, drove 14 hours as a family to my graduation ceremony, I passed my Board Certification exam in Behavior Analysis, and by the end of the year, obtained my business license in Florida. As a reminder to myself, a promise to my clients, and a call back to my mother's words I named my company *LimitLess* Minds. Knowing that we have the power to do great things when we work for it, we are *LimitLess*. We have even greater power and opportunity when we utilize our support systems and are there for each other, our families, and our communities. The power of *LimitLess* to me is that the problems of yesterday, our burdens that we carry, only have the amount of power that we give to them in our tomorrow.

INCLUSION IN OUR COMMUNITY

Despite our differences across communities throughout the globe, there will always be topics that unite us in our shared humanity. One thing close to my heart is kids. Kids are pure joy and innocence; they don't know skin color, brand names, good English, or tax brackets. Kids know ice cream, hide and seek, and tickles and as they grow and get exposed to new challenges and experiences in life, they mold into individuals. If we surround ourselves with good community and we show up, we're helping to enrich the lives around us in our own backyards.

Some of the lives that have come to touch me are from NeuroDivergent learners. Neurodiversity is a natural and valuable form of human diversity. Let's teach our kids and community about DEI, fight stigmas and stereotypes, and promote inclusion in schools and in the workplace. It's been said that kids or special needs kids seem like they are "in their own world," but how often do neighbors and community members go out of their way to make these kids part of their world? How can you be inclusive in your world and community? "Good mornings," smiles, and high fives are free. We can teach our children and family that when we see someone different from us, different doesn't mean bad. Different is an opportunity to learn more about people we share the world with. Teach our community to be a friend by being the example.

REFLECTION QUESTIONS

1. What will you do tomorrow to be sure you "own it and show up"?

2. Do you feel part of your own community? Why do you feel tied to it?

3. How does inclusion look in your own life?

BIOGRAPHY

Cristina was born in San Jose, CA and raised in Miami, FL by her mother from Ecuador and her father from Nicaragua. Through her fiancé and his Cuban family, she solidified her Spanish and now beams Latina pride. She continues living in Miami with her fiancé and French bulldog named Pappi. She looks forward to spreading Latinx Pride to her future children and spreading knowledge on ABA and Neurodiversity throughout her community.

Cristina graduated from Florida International University (FIU) in 2013 with a bachelor's degree in Psychology and concentration in Applied Behavior Analysis (ABA). She started her career in ABA in college, through an internship providing one-on-one treatments with kids with Autism to improve their language and problem-solving skills. In 2018, Cristina graduated with a Master's in Exceptional Student Education (ESE) and ABA, then soon passed the Board Certification exam granting her the title of BCBA- Board Certified Behavior Analyst. She is making an impression in the field and her community through her pediatric therapy company *LimitLess Minds* providing therapy and Early Intervention that changes kids' and families' lives and enables her staff to make a respectable living doing work that comes from the heart, using a science that betters the world and our community.

Cristina Nuñez
info@LLMinds.com
www.LLMinds.com
@LimitLessMinds.ABA on all socials
www.linkedin.com/in/CristinaNunezLLM

Captain Linda Pauwels

Bamboo grove–
Here, too, there's no
Perfection
–Kobayashi Issa (1812)

COURAGE

I was born in San Pedro, a small town in the province of Buenos Aires, Argentina. My father, Jerzy Pfeiffer, was Polish. His father, General Franciszek Pfeiffer, was a unit commander during the Warsaw Uprising. He was captured, sent to Bergen Belsen prisoner of war camp, and later died in exile in London. My grandmother, Tamara Stylinska, was interned in Auschwitz. After surviving captivity, she travelled to Argentina to join my father, who had been sent there during the war.

My mother, Mabel Gaspard, met my father in San Pedro. Her father, Carlos Gaspard, came from a French family and was orphaned as a young child. Gaspard learnt on his own how to read and write, and he is still remembered as a great swimming coach. He was also the first 'health nut' I ever met. Francisca Rodriguez, my mother's mother, emigrated from the Canary

Islands. She was the eldest of six children and her mother died during childbirth, leaving her to raise her younger siblings. She was known as a healer, and her protective nature was passed directly onto me.

My father died at the age of 39, when I was six years old and my brother, Walter, was two. The official cause of death was listed as a heart attack. However, some doubts persisted due to his involvement in political affairs.

Courageously, but without economic means or any other support, my widowed mother emigrated to the United States with two little children. Mom was strong, athletic, and spirited. Although she was a teacher by profession, she could only find menial jobs. When my mom was unable to take care of us, she sent us back to Argentina to live with relatives or other families.

To say my childhood was difficult is an understatement. And as *ferrum ferro acuitur*, this strong-willed, intelligent child became fearless.

TEMPERANCE

One summer, I travelled to Miami to visit my mother. I was 16 at that time and studying to take the entrance exam to the Faculty of Medicine in Buenos Aires. I needed to earn some money, and my mom, who was working at an airline at MIA airport, told me Wardair Canada needed French speaking agents. I was hired, and part of my job was taking flight plans to the pilots. The first time I set foot in a Boeing 747 cockpit, I knew I wanted to fly. I loved the pilots' raw masculine strength and felt the confidence they exuded., At that moment, I was driven by the thought of doing something unthinkable.

Everyone told me it was impossible. I was just a girl who had neither money nor connections. So, I set out to find a way, and ultimately proved them wrong. Since I could not afford to pay for training at a regular flight school, I got two jobs, rented airplanes, and found independent instructors who would help me. I took my private pilot license at 17. That same day in the lobby of the flight school, I met instructor Frederick Pauwels, the man who would later become my husband. I was wearing a t-shirt with "Nice *Côte d'Azur*" and he came over to say his mother was living nearby in Saint-Raphael. We were married a year later, when I was 18 and he was 29.

Frederick was born in Leopoldville, in what was then the Belgian Congo. Tall, square-jawed, strikingly handsome, but complicated, as most pilots tend to be. People were not shy about saying our marriage would not last. Well, it certainly has not been peaches and cream, but here we are, still married forty years later.

Our lives have been weathered and tempered by time, two children, and a full complement of good and bad experiences.

JUSTICE

Early on, as two pilots struggling to build flight time, Frederick and I would each go anywhere we could fly. We were often separated. In 1984, and as was commonly the case, I was the only woman in a pilot class. My friend Charlie and I were hired by commuter airline Air New Orleans. However, they did not get the expected funding and we were promptly furloughed right after completing class. There was a retired military pilot in the class, and he and Charlie got a job at Southern Air Transport, on an L-100, the civilian version of a C-130 military transport.

Unfortunately, that opportunity was not an option for me because I was a woman. Southern Air had been owned by the Central Intelligence Agency, but by that time it was a private company. However, they still had many retired military pilots, no women, and no intention to hire any women. Their worldwide operations could be demanding, and pilots were often away from home for long periods of time.

I was very happy for my friend, though fully incensed by the injustice. I got the number of the secretary to the Director of Operations and called her. I found out that she was Hispanic, so I spoke to her in Spanish and explained that I knew they were hiring pilots and that my friend had been hired, therefore I would like to apply for a position. She laughed: "Linda, they will not hire a woman." I let her know I would be taking a flight to Miami, and would sit on their doorstep until they granted me an interview.

As it came to pass, I obtained an interview and convinced them to hire me. At the age of 21, I was the first woman pilot the company ever hired, as a first officer on the L-100. I reported to class two weeks later, wearing a below the knee dark blue floral dress with a lace collar. The men did not know what to make of me. Much like the relations in the animal kingdom, an Alpha always knows another Alpha. They came to love and respect me.

In what is a job of apprenticeship, these men taught me well. I'll always carry that with me and honor them. Four years later, I became Southern Air's first woman Captain, on a B707. I was 25, and the youngest jet captain in the world.

American Airlines hired me a year later and I have been working with them for 33 years. I then became American's first Latina Captain, and the airline's first Latina Check Airman. Nowadays, I am an instructor and evaluator on the B787. It is most fitting this beautiful airplane is called the "Dreamliner."

WISDOM

Today, my resume details all the different airplanes I am qualified to fly, my education, publications, awards and honors, and many other things I have been fortunate enough to accomplish in life. However, it does not give insight into who I am, or how I filled the hole in my heart that I carried for so many years as a child. For that, the reader will have to take a look at a little poetry book project I titled *Beyond Haiku*.

This is by far my most soulful endeavor. The first book, Pilots Write Poetry, was published in the midst of COVID-19, on December 10, 2020. I am now working on the second, Women Pilots Write Poetry. The third will be Seasons of a Pilot's Life, and the fourth Military Pilots Write Poetry. These books are a shared creative effort, featuring original haiku and short poems by pilots, with illustrations by children of pilots. Proceeds from the books will go to fund aviation scholarships. These books are bringing joy to children and, at the same time, providing the means for pilots to explore their creative side, which often takes a back seat to the rigors of the job.

My own children, Nathalie and Patrick, are now grown-ups. Nathalie attended the United States Naval Academy and is an Intelligence Officer in the Navy. Though her eyesight prevented her from being a military pilot, she still found a way to fly. In March 2021, she became a civilian flight instructor.

Patrick was a rebellious teenager, and almost put us six foot under. He graduated from the University of Maine last year and is a drug and alcohol counselor. He says perhaps one day he will get a Ph.D. in Psychology.

On March 10, 2021, I turned 58. For my birthday, my son Patrick sent me this poem, along with a note that said, "Mom, I want to fly:"

I look into the Sky Blue
That sky that was never the limit
For you
You taught me strength
Never changed your hue
You taught me wisdom
You kept me true
I know our skies
Were never always blue
Just know I love you

REFLECTION QUESTIONS

1. How do we tap into our inner strength?

2. Is resilience innate or can it be developed?

3. How do we cut through the daily noise to begin inching our way towards wisdom?

BIOGRAPHY

Captain Linda Pauwels is an airline pilot. She was hired by American Airlines in 1988 and is presently a Check Airman on the B787 based in DFW. Linda has also been a Check Airman on the A320 and a Flight Engineer Check Airman on the B727. During her more than thirty-year career at American Airlines, she has flown on B727, B757/767, B777, B787, A300, A320, and MD-80, in domestic and international flight operations. Linda is American Airlines' first Latina captain and first Latina Check Airman. She has also served on several local and national committees of the Allied Pilots Association, including Communications, Aeromedical, Training, Safety, and Security.

Prior to joining American Airlines, Linda flew as B707 Captain and L-100 (C-130) First Officer for Southern Air Transport, a Part 121 cargo carrier with worldwide military and civilian contract operations. Linda was the first woman pilot hired at Southern Air Transport and their first female captain. She is listed as the youngest woman cargo jet captain in the world by the International Society of Women Airline Pilots, a distinction she achieved at the age of 25 while flying a B707 for Southern Air Transport.

Born in Argentina, Linda is fluent in Spanish and French. During her time on the Communications Committee, she was called upon to comment on aviation matters by CNN en Español, CNN, Fox News Channel, MSNBC, ABC Nightline, Telemundo, and Univision. She also wrote an aviation issues column, titled *From the Cockpit,* for the Orange County Register.

Linda has degrees in aviation from Miami-Dade College and Embry-Riddle Aeronautical University, and a graduate degree in Education from Azusa Pacific University. She lives in both the Miami and Dallas-Fort Worth areas with her husband, Frederick, a retired airline pilot. They have two adult children, Nathalie and Patrick.

Linda Pauwels
Email: pilots.haiku@gmail.com
IG: @beyondhaiku

Tatiana Quaife

"We need to unlearn that we need to fit in to be successful and relearn that we can only be truly successful as our bright authentic selves."

When I was a little girl, I wanted to be an executive at a big company. I do not know why, but I would walk around my house wearing my mom high heels and holding my dad's briefcase pretending I was going to work. I know most kids have more exciting dreams like being a firefighter or an astronaut, but that was my only goal. The amazing thing is that even though Brazil is a very patriarchal country, my dad believed in me and told me I could be and do whatever I wanted. He believed that the world was going to be female one day and he helped me get ready for that.

While I was empowered and encouraged to reach for the stars, I also learned at a very young age that the world was not equal (YET) and that meant I would face a lot of challenges and difficulties to achieve my dream, but I was both driven and determined.

I realized I had to study super hard, get the best grades

possible, go to the best schools, and get the best jobs. I needed to follow a required path to get to the top, so I even moved to the US all by myself to get better education and start my career in Corporate America.

Then, I experienced discrimination and racism in my first job out of school, and that crushed. Mistakenly, I decided to change the way I acted, talked, looked, and behaved in order to fit in and be successful. I even worked extremely hard to hide my accent, dialed down my passionate personality, wore more black and white clothes (getting rid of my colorful Brazilian pieces). However, I found the way to keep some of my bright colorful personality by wearing bold and colorful Brazilian necklaces.

Also, by looking up and around in Corporate America, I discovered I needed to lead more like a man in order to be respected, so I became more assertive, learned to hide my emotions, started to take wider places at tables and using war terms in my vocabulary.

After some time, I had completely morphed myself to pave my way to success. This "fitting in" approach seemed to be quite effective in many ways: I was performing well, moving up the ladder, and feeling really proud of the results. However, deep inside, I was miserable. I was exhausted, stressed, overwhelmed, and felt stuck. I did not like the image of Tatiana that the mirror reflected having lost my spark or passion. I had lost my light.

ANSWERING LIFE'S WAKE UP CALL

I was in complete denial, so I kept sucking it up and pushing through things until I had a HUGE wakeup call. I was diagnosed with early stage breast cancer, which shocked me to the core. I am happy to say that I am healthy now and I think cancer helped me realize I needed to stop and make deep changes.

I learned (clearly the hard way) I cannot be truly happy or fulfilled if I am not true to myself. I had been wearing so many different masks pretending to be someone else for so long that I almost got lost in the path.

Through self-reflection, I realized that I needed to redefine what success should look like for me on my own terms. But, before I could rise up, a deep inner journey to heal my wounds was required.

DIVING DEEP INTO OUR INNER JOURNEY CAN BE QUITE MESSY

To tell the truth, I first went through a phase of anger because I thought I was doing everything right to climb the corporate ladder. Goodness! I was freaking exhausted, always chasing, striving, and never feeling good enough. After digging really deep, I had a big aha moment as I realized that the masks I was wearing were the symptoms. It was not just about taking the masks off, I needed to explore my inner self to find the root cause.

I became aware of my mindset or, more transparently, the ruthless and unchecked stories I was telling myself. The huge non-stop drama— or as I prefer to say "novelas"— with all that fear and self-doubt as the big star of my life. The self-criticism, or impostor syndrome voice, was driving myself crazy. Although

I found some ways to effectively manage all the mind drama and become the author of my "novelas," I still needed to dive deeper to get to the real root cause.

So, I kept digging inwards, like an archeologist excavating, and while it was often painful, messy and frustrating to adventure into the depths within me, I knew I had to be very persistent to break free.

After many months digging, I finally got it! I realized that I had been working so damn hard and giving all of me to achieve success because I believed my career accomplishments would validate my worthiness. My insatiable desire for professional growth and the constant need for external validation were driven by a deeply-seated fear or limiting belief that I was not actually good enough.

I had learned somehow or picked up from society that girls or women were not good enough and that I was not worthy as a woman. It was not until I could face and feel the weight and heaviness of this limiting belief and once and for all uproot it that I was really able to unleash my full potential.

It seems I had a foot on the accelerator pushing down as hard as I could—pedal to the metal—but not quite moving forward; I felt stuck because I did not realize that I was simultaneously putting the other foot on the brake pedal—that was my limiting belief of not being good enough. I first needed to let it go so I could actually move forward smoothly.

I finally learned that I could not achieve the true growth and fulfillment I have been looking for in the outside because nobody, no job, or promotion could give that to me. The growth, the validation, the power, the recognition, the acceptance and the love that I was so desperately searching for were all within myself. The power was within me. It has always been within me, I had just given it away and I did not know it.

I learned that letting go of limiting beliefs is a journey of self-awareness, deep compassion, and insane courage. We need courage to let go of belief systems that have been with us since we were kids because they are no longer useful and just hold us back. Since wearing these masks has kept us safe, taking them off can be really scary, what if it backfires?

The truth is that most of us are afraid of ourselves, of the power and magic that we all have within us. There is this beautiful and thought-provoking quote from Marianne Williamson that I keep at hand: "Our deepest fear is that we are powerful beyond measure. It is out light, not our darkness, that most frightens us." So, ask yourself what you would do, how you would feel, who you would be if you were not afraid. Who would you be and how would you feel without these masks?

We ultimately need the courage to be truly seen, to show and bring our true authentic selves to work and life, to step into and unleash our inner power. But after so many years or decades wearing masks, diming our light, silencing our voices and fitting in, relearning to be our true authentic selves takes time, practice, and baby steps. Baby step by baby step, we build momentum and rebuild our inner confidence to shine brightly.

IGNITING A LIGHT RIPPLE EFFECT AS LEADERS

The truth is that going through this deep inner journey changed me as a human being, as a professional, and as a leader. Leading as a vulnerable, authentic, whole-hearted leader was a game-changer for my team and our culture.

From my own personal journey, I learned it is a LOT easier for people to be their authentic selves and bring their full selves to work when they feel safe, encouraged, and empowered to do so. In my experience, that comes down from the leaders. If leaders create that culture and environment, people can be their full selves with confidence and trust, and without fear.

I think most leaders would certainly agree to the idea that we should all feel like we belong and can be ourselves at work; however, the majority of leaders do not realize many people certainly do not feel that way. I have had many open, uncomfortable and vulnerable conversations around Diversity and Inclusion recently and that has been perhaps the biggest surprise and shock among leaders.

As leaders, we need to be aware that all our team members are not machines but human beings going through their own inner journeys, with inner challenges, and barriers to overcome and break free from.

This change, which goes from "feeling like you needed to fit in to be successful" to "realizing you can only be truly successful as your authentic self" is massive. So, what can we do to create a culture where everyone feels like they belong and can bring their full selves? We can start by leading by example: being authentic, vulnerable, humble human leaders. As I opened up and put my guard down, I showed my team they could do the same and we connected on a much deeper human level.

We need to create a culture of trust and psychological safety where people are not afraid of speaking up, trying new things, and even making mistakes because they know we have their backs.

Ultimately, we need to show that we care for them not just as employees but as human beings and that we are committed to not only their professional growth but to their personal inner growth as well. That will ignite a fire within them that we have not seen before.

Since I have taken off my mask and started leading as my bright, authentic self, something magical happened: other people saw the spark, they saw it was possible to let go of their masks too.

The truth is that any change needs to start within us, within each of us. We cannot change the world, but we CAN change ourselves, heal ourselves, and relearn to shine our bright authentic lights. And when we do that, we lead in the most powerful way, we lead by example, others see it, and are inspired to go in their inner journeys as well. Then, together we create a light ripple effect at work.

REFLECTION QUESTIONS

1. What kind of masks you have been wearing, who you have been pretending to be or not be?

2. Who would you be or how would you feel without these masks? What is wearing these masks costing you?

3. Would you like to take your masks off and shine brightly as your true self?

BIOGRAPHY

Tatiana Quaife is a purpose-driven executive, inspirational speaker and thought-leader using her authentic voice and experiences to inspire Corporate America professionals to unlock and unleash their true potential from within themselves.

With over twelve years of leadership experience as a Latina executive with The Walt Disney Company and Procter & Gamble, she personally experienced the pressure and challenges many professionals face in their journeys to success.

Growing up in Corporate America, Tatiana learned that she needed to fit into a specific mold to be successful; so, she changed herself to achieve her dream of being an executive at a big company.

Tatiana began to feel the cost that this "fitting in" approach had. Feeling burnout, stressed, and overwhelmed, Tatiana knew there had to be a new and better way of achieving professional success.

Even though Tatiana faced many external challenges, she learned her greatest battles were actually inside herself with her mindset being often her worst enemy.

Tatiana went on a profound inner journey to create change from within herself. She devised a system for doing the "inner work" of unlearning and relearning, so she could break through from the inside out.

After realizing that others were also struggling with similar difficulties, Tatiana felt compelled to share her journey openly and vulnerably. She turned to public speaking, writing, and coaching to inspire and empower others also to do their own "inner work," so they could unleash their authentic magic within.

Tatiana Quaife
FB, IG, Twitter, LinkedIn: @TatianaQuaife
www.tatianaquaife.com

HIS PLAN, MY ACTIONS, AND THE DETOURS

Adriana Rozo-Angulo

"My character is only the result of the experiences, changes, and trials I have encountered during the years and how I have reacted to that every second of my life"

For as long as I can remember, my life has been filled with changes and experiences, and those in some way marked my journey. However, I am a firm believer that each person forges its own destiny and that your past does not determine your future. Instead, your actions—and more important, your reactions—to every situation can keep you on or deviate you from your path. I also know that if you carry your GPS all the time, you will not get lost, no matter how many times you take the wrong path.

When I was a child, my dad used to travel a lot for work, and I founded business trips exciting. Then, my mom also started travelling for work, but not within Colombia like dad, but to other countries. Unlike my father, she used to take my two sisters and me along with her, that was her number one condition. I was amazed every time we had the chance to take any trip with her because I loved changing landscapes and experiencing new situations. Looking back, I can realize that all those experiences prepared me to be the change agent I am now. I learned to adapt to circumstances and take the best of each situation. Just a tiny little thing that captured my interest out of the whole experience was enough to get on board without hesitation. This is still the case. When I must deal with change, I always try to find a benefit, regardless how small it can be, and focus on it. When you focus on the benefit, it is easier to manage the aspects that take us out of our comfort zone or the ones we do not enjoy that much.

I started planning my career when I was in middle school. I loved to spend my time after school at my mom's office. Usually, my tasks involved stamping invoices and filing documents. I still remember how important I felt just doing so. I would rather choose the office or the bank when playing with my sisters. Being a Manager, a Director, and then a CEO were the natural positions I expected in the forthcoming future. In my view, the simple equation to achieve my goals was Passion + Study + Hard Work = Success.

MY PLAN

Many things happened during my school years. Among others, my parents divorced—which was an overly complicated time with many changes and drama. Despite being trapped in an emotional turmoil, I kept my eyes on my goal and my easy view of success at that time. I deflected the problems by studying and reading as an escape. I enjoyed learning so much that I became a dedicated reader—and used to spend hours reading at the library when not in class. My enthusiasm for books led me to discover my passion for philosophy, which connected with my internal inquiries with respect to the nature of being and existence. I remember my mom was a little worried about my preferences, including Camus, Sartre, Nietzsche, and Schopenhauer. Such literature is not exactly the first choice you desire for your 15-year-old daughter, but that I can tell now that I have a 15-year-old boy. I graduated at age 16 with a student record full of "As". That great achievement was part of my success plan. My equation was simply working out!

But, guess what? I soon realized that life cannot be reduced to a simple young-dream equation, and that plans never come free of challenges, trials, detours, and unexpected obstacles. Yet, I had to acknowledge that what I thought as my plan, in fact was His plan. And then it was on me to decide what actions and reactions to put into practice not to keep me away from the path.

When I graduated from college, I felt the huge responsibility of starting to build my own life, not as a mere passenger but as the driver. I was then "writing my story." I have always had an adventurous spirit and then I was up to the audacious trip; nonetheless, I was not completely ready for the drive tests and definitively not aware of the road signs. I believe that at some point all of us get to this stage in life where we think we know everything and can conquer the word by ourselves because we have the perfect plan.

I launched into the adventure of the career and the family almost simultaneously, believing I could have everything under control. In my eagerness to conquer the world though, I forgot the importance of carrying a GPS—that gadget that would show me the route and help me if I got lost or detoured. Then, I came upon a closed road and did not know where to go or how to find the way back. Now, years gone by, I can assure that fearful moment of confusion was my first divine detour. God works in mysterious ways. He puts traffic signs we usually ignore because of the hurry. We truly believe we know where we are going and that we have the control and the perfect plan. It is important to create a strategy, to believe in ourselves, and to be confident; however, we need to be prepared for disruptions and to change the game at any given moment. Furthermore, we need to understand that if we must start a new game, that does not mean we were no capable or that we have failed.

FINDING THE GPS AND GETTING INTO THE NEW ROAD

With no intention to minimize the problems, the struggles, the frustration, and the confusion we may all face throughout our lives, let me assert that if we take the suitable gear, acute devices, and a precise mindset, our journey will be easier, more pleasant, and we will definitely arrive at our destination at the end of the day. I love the metaphor of the road trip to illustrate my life. It would be obviously faster and statistically safer if we take a plane, but the treasure of the experiences and the landscapes would be missed. The lessons to be learned and the wonders that a detour can give you are priceless.

After my first closed road, I started looking for directions and found the GPS that has been guiding me since then: my faith, and the certainty that even if I cannot see it, God is working on His plan for my life. I may not know the how or the when, but He will help me overcome the obstacles giving me the confidence I need to continue. It is faith what gives us the courage to plunge into new business, commitments, adventures, and the fearless spirit to ambition bigger goals.

As it happens with any new journey, I started with a lot of enthusiasm. I did my research, surrounded myself with people that could help me not to deviate from the path. I took my GPS with me, so nothing could go wrong. Again, I was on my road to success! But the truth has nothing to do with reality. Success does not only depend on skills and capabilities; faith alone cannot guarantee a life without hurdles.

Problems would come and not go; my success equation was not working at all; my knowledge was not enough to get me to the desired stop. It was more difficult being a woman and a Latina. I had to prove I was twice as competent as others to get what I deserved. I was not able to find balance between my family life and my job. I often felt guilty for not attending school readings, or not being part of the PTA, or cooperating with my children's school in any way. Right now, my older son is just a semester away from college graduation and I know I made the right decision. I might have not been the always-present-mom, but I taught them by example, that if you persevere, work hard, always help others, and do not lose faith and seek after God's guidance, you will certainly meet your goals.

MY ACTIONS AND REACTIONS

There is one thing that has been constant along the path: results and the delays have always been directly affected by my actions and reactions.

In 2018, I was in a good place professionally. I had met many of my goals and proved myself twice in two different areas where I gradually got to the position of Director. I already had what I wanted—or at least I used to think so. Cultural messages can be tricky enough to make us assume certain circumstances as the regular and acceptable rule in our path to success. I had a lot of responsibilities, a lot of stress, I was traveling most of the time and away from my family; however, I thought I was doing great. By then, unfortunately (though now I can heartly say "fortunately"), my managers were not happy with the results and remove me from the big project I was involved in and assigned me to a different area. I kept my position; however, my responsibilities changed completely. I was devastated, and on denial, I could not believe that after all those years of sacrifice and hard work, they would believe I was not good enough. At that moment I was not internally aware of detours, actions, and reactions... I just felt frustrated and at a dead-end in my career. My faith was also tested. I prayed a lot for those things I used to consider important at that moment, and things I could not control. My job and career were not part of those prayers. I believed I had control over my career; my passion, my studies, and hard work had taken me to what I considered my final destination. It was nothing but the equation! But that was my huge mistake. I should have surrendered my career to God. In the end, I realized that in fact we have the control, but only on how we react to a certain situation and on what actions we take as a consequence.

The pandemic we are currently facing is a good example. We are all indisputably living it, though we are not all under the same circumstances. We have witnessed people and companies making a huge turn to help other people, reinventing themselves, pursuing old dreams for the first time. Other people, however, decided to stand still and just wait for the assistance of the government or any other agency or organization, just waiting, blaming on others, or criticizing.

So, what should we do when we encounter a dead-end in our journey? Something that helps me is to break the scheme down into phases:

- **Phase 1:** It is right and also important to allow yourself to feel frustration, anger, and to wonder why; nevertheless, you should not stand numb. Always move forward. Trust your faith and trust His word—where you will find the tools you need to overcome the situation.

- **Phase 2:** Redirect, do not get paralyzed, look for the detour signs, and resume the journey. The key at this phase is to learn. What lesson can you get from this experience? What can you do to identify the road signs next time?

- **Phase 3:** Be the light that guides others. Now that you know the path and have learned the lessons, share that knowledge, inspire others, help them with their journey.

The year 2020 has been difficult for everyone. In my case, however, it was also the year in which lots of new doors have opened. In my search for ways to help other people, I discovered Hispanic Star and now I can say I am proudly working as a Leader of the New Jersey Hub. This organization helped me expand my network with excellent connections that showed me a world of possibilities and opportunities. For instance, this is my second collaboration as author, and I published my own book called *The Buoyant Business* in March. I re-launched the consulting company I have founded with my husband nine years ago, and I am still working at my corporate position.

The advantage is I have more time for my family. I have learned to manage and keep a balance in my life where I can work, enjoy my family, help people... and I am faithful to my dreams! This year I have once more proved to myself that a detour is not the end of the road, but the start of a new one. God's plans for your life can be amazing! Just be patient because our timing is not God's timing.

REFLECTION QUESTIONS

1. Do you have a balanced life and are you enjoying it?

2. Do you have a life purpose? Are you following your dreams?

3. Are you living your life to the fullest possible extent?

BIOGRAPHY

Adriana Rozo-Angulo is a passionate leader, strategist, and change agent. She is Director of Operations at Menasha and is currently working with the Business Transformation team. Adriana is also the President of MAS Connections, a business consultancy firm she cofounded in 2011. She is a Lean Six Sigma Black Belt professional and holds several certifications in the manufacturing and medical device industry.

During her 20 years in the industry, Adriana realized that one of the main factors that affects companies of any size is the "Not Applicable" process, idea, and mindset. Her strategic and operational expertise, combined with her lean six sigma background, allows her to promptly identify these situations and create a simpler and sustainable strategy.

Adriana is the New Jersey Hub Leader for The Hispanic Star, an organization under We Are All Human. She is a member of the Advisory Board of Seton Hall University for the "Transformative Leadership in Disruptive Times" executive certificate program. Adriana is the author of the book The Buoyant Business and coauthor of the book *Hispanic Star Rising*. She is also a certified EXMA speaker.

Adriana lives in NJ with her husband Miguel, her two children, Sebastian and Matthew, and her 2 dogs.

Adriana Rozo-Angulo
(908) 721-7535
adriana@mas-conections.com
www.mas-connections.com
LinkedIn: adrianarozoangulo
IG: @adrianarozoangulo

Eliuth Sanchez

"You can't go back and change the beginning, but you can start where you are and change the ending." C. S. Lewis

My name is Eliuth Sanchez and I am 42 years old. When I thought that I had fulfilled all my personal and professional goals, suddenly life put me in front of a hurricane that turned everything upside down and left me in the complete darkness, full of fear and uncertainty. In the year 2020, significant events occurred in my life that forced me to prove myself how strong and resilient I am.

I LOST MY FATHER IN 2020

In May 2020, I had to face the loss of my father. I still remember the last time I saw my dad taking him to the airport for his trip back to Mexico. He came to this country like all Latinos who immigrate to the United States looking for a better future for his family. He worked for 30 years in the same factory until the day of his retirement, which he was very enthusiastic about because, at last, he would return to live in Mexico City where I was born. I am the youngest of five brothers, three boys and two girls. I still remember my father's sacrifice of getting up at 4 a.m. in the morning to go to work. Unfortunately, in May, he had an operation in Mexico and did not recover. The worst thing was that we could not travel to properly say goodbye to him due to the Covid-19 situation. We had to agree to send him the last goodbye through technology. My elder sister was in charge of his farewell with that courage that she always shows us. She made up her mind to travel and take care of the funeral. His departure left me an immense emptiness and a lesson of how fragile life is.

CHICAGO MY NEW LIFE

I arrived in Chicago when I was 11 years old. I was too young to understand how far we were from our country, Mexico, but I knew that after several years, we would finally be back together as a family. As I was the youngest, my elder sister made sure that my only priority was school. My siblings had to work hard and make many sacrifices with my parents so that I would have a better future. They were clear that education could offer me better opportunities. I was always very fond of school. It was very difficult at first because I did not speak or read English, but I learned it very quickly. I graduated from grammar school with honors, I finished high school with honors, and I had the opportunity to attend college because I received several scholarships that help cover my education.

ACHIEVING ALL MY PROFESSIONAL GOALS

In the last year of high school when I had to decide what I would study, I took a journalism class and, only after some weeks, I was the editor for my high school magazine. When I took this class, I felt in love with it, and I realized I had to study something related to the media. In 2001, I got my bachelor's degree in Marketing Communications from Columbia College Chicago. This was one of my first accomplishments that made my family proud, as I was the first one to receive a university degree. Three years after graduation, I achieved one of my most desired goals: to work in the field of my profession. I had the opportunity to work for the Chicago Tribune for 10 years in the Hoy newspaper, the Spanish edition. I started as an assistant to the national sales department, climbing up to become the supervisor of the classifieds sales department. Being part of the Chicago Tribune has been one of the best experiences in my life and where I met the most incredible people who were my great mentors in the Communications industry.

CHOOSING THE BUSINESS PATH

While working for the Chicago Tribune, I opened Latin Plate Catering & Events, a company that offers food service, waiters, decoration, and event planning. My first clients were in the Latin market providing our services to *Quinceañeras*, Weddings, and Birthday parties. There, I found other of my passions and I could put into practice my experience in sales and customer services that I had been gathering for more than 10 years. In 2018, I decided to leave the corporate world to devote myself full time to Latin Plate Catering. It was a very difficult decision because I did not have any experience as an entrepreneur, but I trusted in this project and decided to run the risk. It was not easy at all to make my way in the events industry, yet all along this way, I met incredible people who believed in me and gave me the opportunity to coordinate their special events. The most gratifying thing was at the end of each event when the clients were happy with our food and event planning services. That encouraged me to continue with this adventure.

GROWTH OF LATIN PLATE CATERING & EVENTS

After several years of rendering our services to the Hispanic community, my next goal was to bring my services to corporate companies in the city of Chicago. It was in 2019 when I entered into an association that would open the doors for me to serve lunches in the best companies in Chicago, such as the Willis Tower building. With this opportunity, we had an unimaginable growth: we were preparing 1000 lunches per week and we obtained recognition from our clients as the best Latin food. We had a busy year and were hired to serve the Christmas dinner for Chicago Mayor Lori E. Lightfoot and her staff. It was an honor to be part of this prestigious event.

REINVENTING MYSELF AS A BUSINESSWOMAN DURING THE PANDEMIC

Latin Plate was vanishing in front of my eyes; a job of more than 12 years had completely been brought to a halt by the Covid-19. Those were very difficult months due to the situation of the pandemic and, especially, because I had no idea how I could survive financially since my only source of income was the catering. When I found out that the government would give help to small businesses, I filled out all the possible applications with the hope of receiving some kind of support to be able to pay the rent for my commercial kitchen because I knew that, if I lost it, I would no longer have where to work to continue preparing the food. It was frustrating not to receive any response and I realized that there was a clear inequality for small and minority-owned companies. My business coach Rowan Richards from Allies for Community Business organization continued to encourage me not to give up and soon the answers from the grants began to arrive. At that time, I knew I had to innovate since there was no scheduled date for the offices and events to return to normal activities. In the midst of a pandemic, I decided to open my long-awaited healthy café & protein bar. I went back to the neighborhood where I grew up in Wicker Park to open the healthy café and protein bar. Focused on "guilt-free" protein-based snacks, protein-packed coffees, and antioxidant-rich supplement smoothies and teas, World Nutrition filled a gap in the Wicker Park area. This is a very lively community. They take care of themselves. They go running, exercise, and do long walks. I love and enjoy what I do, that it does not feel like work; besides, we are also helping people with healthier alternatives for their daily routine.

In August 2020, I found the perfect place. For two non-stop tiring months, I worked to build the place and on Saturday October 10, 2020, it was the grand opening. The café replaced a Jimmy John's and the Alderman Daniel La Spata was extremely happy to support our business. He attended the ceremony and did the honor of cutting the ribbon for the grand opening. This day was filled with emotions as I was achieving a dream of having my first brick and mortar business location. I was also nervous because we were in a community to serve the Anglo market and, as a Latina, I did not know what the reaction would be like, but I was pleasantly surprised to have all the support of the community as they gave me a warm welcome.

I am the first woman in my family to start a business and, now, to run a café. Undoubtedly, I owe this success to my family, to my friends, to all the people who have guided me in my professional career, and now in the business world.

MAKING THE HARDEST DECISION OF MY LIFE

As I am writing these paragraphs of my beginnings, my professional life, my achievements, and my entrepreneurial steps at the same time, I am also taking the most difficult decision of my life: ending my marriage of almost 20 years. There are situations that we go through in life we cannot find a reasonable explanation for and this is an example. But even with pain, sadness and fear, I understand that there are circumstances in life that we need to undergo. My position as to this situation is to trust in God and strongly believe that wonderful things will come for my three children and myself. I thank every day for our health and for having them. They are my engine to never give up.

MY MOST IMPORTANT ROLE: BEING A MOTHER

I have the fortune of being a mom of three amazing children. The first Montserrat, who is 19 years old, she is in her first year at the University. My greatest accomplishment is watching my daughter study at DePaul University. I have always taught her about the importance of education to achieve all her goals and to stand out in this country.

My second daughter, Dayanara, 14, who is a very dedicated student, always with honors, she is currently is in 8th grade, and the youngest, Giancarlo, 11, who came to complete my family and filled me with a lots of love, he is very talented at drawing.

They are my strength and the best gift that God gave me. They are the reason why I cannot afford to give up even when life gets harder. After all this storytelling of my life and what I have had to face, I have decided to move on in search of my path and without losing focus on my goals and dreams; but the most important thing is to be grateful, enjoy, laugh, and love. Also, my great qualities have revealed to myself, such as how strong and resilient I am without surrendering. If I fall down one-hundred times, I rise up one-hundred and one. It has not been easy, but I have always looked for a way out and asked for help, when necessary.

I understand that I cannot go back and change the beginning because life is full of good and not-so-good experiences that have helped me mature and bring a different meaning into my story, starting from where I am in the present, in order to be able to change the ending.

REFLECTION QUESTIONS

1. Have you ever felt despaired because of a critical situation going through?

2. Have you thought about changing the focus to find the way out?

3. How much do you trust in yourself? Isn't it high time to start?

BIOGRAPHY

Eliuth Sanchez is an entrepreneur with 13+ years in the food industry. She is the founder and CEO of Latin Plate Catering and Events Corp and Co-Founder of World Nutrition. She is the first woman in her family to own a business.

While pursuing a successful career in corporate sales organizations, the idea of starting her own business took hold. So, 12 years ago she took the leap. But it was in 2018 that she decided to commit full-time to Latin Plate.

Latin Plate has allowed her to combine her passion and expertise in event planning, sales, and customer service. Originally, she began the catering business within the Hispanic community by catering to weddings, cotillions, and birthdays. But she had a broader vision and wanted to provide services and of course, food, to a wider market.

In 2020 she opened her first brick & mortar Café/Protein Bar in the Wicker Park Community offering delicious desserts and foods but with a healthy twist. She looks forward to continuing growing the catering business, plans to open a second Café/Protein Bar place and pursuing an MBA in Business Administration.

She has earned several recognitions and awards as professional and entrepreneur.

Eliuth Sanchez
Latin Plate Catering & Events Corp
FB: Latin Plate Catering
IG: @Latinplate
World Nutrition
2029 W Division St Chicago IL 60622
FB: World Nutrition Smoothie and Juice Bar
IG: @Worldnutritionchi

THE STREETS, THE UNIVERSITY OF LIFE

Marilú Serrano

"Life may be wonderful, or it may be only tears; it is just up to you how you want to live"

"Two limes for one peso," I used to say to the people who would open the door of their houses in Jalpa, Zacatecas, Mexico, as I offered them my product being just a six-year-old peddler. My eyes sparkled with enthusiasm and just kept smiling with the full conviction I was selling the most delicious limes grown at home.

FROM PRINCESS TO CINDERELLA

My grandmother Maury—my mom's mother—said to me: "Dear, you have to learn to make your living soon because I will not live much longer, and your grandad is not here to care of you. What are you going to do with your life without a mother or a father to protect you?"

Maury simply wanted to teach me to be on my own; to pass on to me the values and morals necessary to cope with life from an early age. I really get now! She gave the most valuable gifts: the pillars on which to build a good and balanced life.

Daddy Felix Serrano—mi *abuelito*—was my whole everything; he was my protector, my hero, the most important person in my life. Suddenly, he was no longer there. I was not able to puzzle out the meaning of death; I was just a six-year-old girl. I felt lost and confused when he died. He loved me as a daughter.

Sadly, my life went from pink to grey after he died. I was physically and emotionally abused by an aunt—the youngest daughter of my grandparents, who would frequently slap and beat me. And, besides selling limes in the streets, my grandmother had me do the household chores. I recall I walked for over an hour to return home from school carrying a heavy book bag to find her waiting for me so that I washed the dishes because "dinner had to be ready for sale."

We had a stand in the front of the house where we sold *tacos dorados*. That was our family income. My grandma often told me: "You are my feet and my hands." She suffered from rheumatism and it was very difficult for her to stand up once she had sat.

THE ADVENTURE TO THE LAND OF THE OPPORTUNITY

Desperation upon such mistreatment drove to leave my hometown at the age of 14 with the wishful thinking of getting to know my mother better—who had just paid me a visit a couple of times after she left when I was three.

There were these two neighbor ladies who offered to take me to the United States to join my mother. I planned my escape for over a month hiding my suitcase in the barn. I kept that secret from my grandma because I was afraid of Leticia—my wicked aunt. From time to time, Leticia would go out from home for a while leaving me to babysit her elder daughter. Fortunately, when the time came to join my neighbors, Leticia was out of town.

A few days before I ran away I told my grandma I would go with the Olmos ladies—my neighbors—to see my mom in the United States. I asked her for her blessing, which was the best gift I could have taken with me. Now, I feel proud of myself for having taken such a courageous decision of asking her permission in such way although I was just 14.

My heart fills with nostalgia when I remember Maury standing out of the house looking at me without believing her eyes as I departed in the taxi, though deep-down in her she knew she could not deny me the chance to meet my mother and go find a better life.

The Olmos ladies had promised they would take me to live with my mother, but they just left me at the border in Tijuana with some unknown people that were going to take me to the United States. The ladies separated from me but would keep my suitcase with all my clothes and an address book after a grandchild of theirs attempted to run away. I was left alone without money or food. Luckily, I believe in miracles and the power of almighty God that always has angels to protect, guide and help me. There was always somebody to feed or assist me on the way.

There was this guy, especially, who took special care of me

as an older brother while we were crossing to the United States through Tijuana. I was in a group of over 20 people among men, women, and children; however, this guy was all the time by my side holding my hand and telling me what to do.

We lived lots of experiences together, such as tramping over large ponds. One time, the men in charge (the *coyotes*) told us to undress so as not to get sick, but I did not obey because I felt really embarrassed of being naked. They were right though; I got a very high fever and it was this guy who asked the coyotes for medicine to cure me. He also hid me in a whole when a helicopter of the border patrol flew over our heads at a very short distance. We were taken into a tunnel and then behind the seats of a pick-up truck. I was so young I felt all that like a movie, more adventurous than dangerous. I never saw that guy again— whose name I still do not know—but I always think about him as a protective angel sent by God to be my shelter.

REUNION WITH MY MOTHER

Finally, after several days sharing with all these unknown people, it came the miracle. I was finally and successfully crossed to the promised land. I just so happened that I remembered one of the phone numbers in the address book left in the suitcase I had lost that helped as contact number so that they could take me with my mom.

At the end of such risky adventure, I was there with my mother in Oxnard. Nonetheless, when I saw the circumstances in which she was living, I got scared. I could see nothing else but violence. My mom and her children were battered by her husband. I decided my chances could be better; thus, I left.

My options were limited at that moment. It was not possible to continue with my neighbor ladies, who were living in Oxnard, California. I would definitely not stay with my mother. So, I asked an aunt if she would let me stay with her in Chicago.

BEING A TEENAGER IN CHICAGO

I am truly thankful to my aunt Marina who provided me with accommodation and registered me at school. She also made me work at a factory packing candy. I was just 14.

Then, I decided to move with another aunt for a short time. My grandmother had come to visit me—she had a visa—after a teacher called her telling I might be at risk of becoming part of a gang and waste my life if she did not prevent it. After a while, my aunt kicked us off—I do not know even why. We were sitting on the stairs outside my aunt's house carrying just some plastic bags as baggage when I asked my grandma: "Ma, where are we going now?" Her answer was: "Do not worry, my dear. I will work it out." And then we went to live temporarily in the attic of one of my grandma's nephews.

By then, I studied in the morning and work as a checker at a supermarket in the afternoon. Meanwhile, as I worked, I tried to find out among customers about furnished apartments to move with granny. No long after that, we were living in a small apartment in the area of Villita, Chicago. I still can remember the gang that used to gather just in front of the window of my bedroom that made me sleep all curled up in fear. Once again, God's gentle hand was present in my life.

A LIFE OF WORK AND SATISFACTION

I have had many different jobs at factories, supermarkets, restaurants, cleaning floors and toilets, always trying to exceed my own expectations.

I decided to quit my job at the supermarket and started to work in a bank. Besides, as I never forgot the skills I have earned at selling limes, I started selling goods door to door in the streets of Chicago.

A woman called Juanita Ledezma told me about the Shaklee Corporation—a prime health and wellness products company. She was so kind at encouraging me to try it by saying: "You, girl, are very talented. You will make all your dreams come true, whether travelling the world, winning a car, buying a house, but mainly having plenty of health."

She convinced me immediately, basically after she told me I could get a car and have my own house. All her words sounded terrific, especially as they were told by a former homeless. Without hesitation, I asked her what I should do. She told me that all I needed was a testimony of myself to share with others. Just that to start building my own customer and distributors' network to generate an income for the rest of my life.

LIFE IS A BEAUTIFUL BIKE RIDE

I got down to business and I managed to have my car in just six months after visiting many customers on foot, walking long hours down the cold streets of Chicago or riding my bicycle in the summer, to deliver my products. Step by step, I kept on upgrading my status as I accomplished goals, including having my own house at age 25, travelling the world after winning over 35 trips and getting eight cars as rewards.

I HAVE ALWAYS DREAMED OF MY OWN FAMILY

My biggest success has been getting married to Luis M. García and having my children Luis—23 years old—and Andrés—20 years old—who are the loves of my life. I hope my stories may serve as inspiration to my children, my grandchildren, and the future generations.

My husband and I have invested in a series of properties, including a building in Cicero— where I set up my company Centro Vida Sana—with apartments and offices for rent, and an events room I manage.

Who could have bet that an innocent girl selling limes in the streets of her hometown would learn such key lessons to build a full and plenty life of success?

Now, my next big goal is to pass my message to other women to stimulate them to pursue their dreams no matter how much distress they have suffered in life. God has a purpose for each of us that is always amazing and up to what we can handle. It is just a question of faith. Believe in God because He is the loving father who furnish us with all we need to make our dreams come true.

GRATITUDE CHANGES EVERYTHING

Allow me a special thanks to my aunt Maria Serrano for always supporting my grandma and me despite not leaving in the same place. She has always kept an eye on us and provided for our needs. She was the one who bought me my first brassiere when I was a teenager—at a time when talking about a girl's physical changes was somehow tabu, she stood by me without asking or saying anything. I love you, auntie, and I appreciate enormously your unconditional love and help. I know now you are an angel still taking care of me from Heaven.

With a humble heart I say I feel honored and thankful for the possibility of joining in *Today's Inspired Latina Volume IX* as author. No words are enough to thank you, Gaby Gomez, my dear friend, who has pushed me to write my story. I hope I can inspire others to take the plunge.

Above all, I thank God and every day I entrust my life to Him to serve his commands. To You be all the glory.

REFLECTION QUESTIONS

1. What do you do when things do not go as planned?

2. What helps you keep focused on the accomplishment of your goals?

3. What do you need to put into work to have your dreams come true?

BIOGRAPHY

Marilú Serrano has worked in Shaklee for over thirty years building a huge network that has helped her earn her income and much more selling remotely through digital tools and social networks. She offers training and classes to business and product leaders.

She is the CEO and owner of Centro Vida Sana and also runs and manages an events room in the same premises.

Marilú and her husband are partners at Sega Propiedades, a business devoted to the purchase, refurbishment, sale, and construction of properties. They also have apartments and units for rent.

Her purpose is to inspire and motivate women to keep physically and financially healthy, and to discover new options to live the lives of their dreams not seeing money as an obstacle to achieve their goals.

Marilú Serrano
(773) 9838710
Mariluserrano10@gmail.con
pws.shaklee.com/vidasana

Lucy Vazquez-Gonzalez

"I fought for my rights. Now I fight for the rights of others, giving a voice to the voiceless."

It is sometimes hard for me to understand how far I have come. My path to where I am today—the owner of my own successful law firm, respected in my community, with a happy and secure family—was a long and rocky one, but I value every bump and pitfall, for without them I would not be the person I am now.

EARLY CHALLENGES

My childhood was fraught with tragedy and danger. During my entire childhood, I suffered physical and sexual abuse by my stepfather, a violent alcoholic who terrorized our family on a daily basis. While decades have passed since that time, I still remember his brutality like it was yesterday.

My mother posed another challenge. She suffered from her own serious deficiencies and failed entirely to protect me from my stepfather's abuse. I loved her nonetheless, and tried to protect her from her husband, often getting in between them and bearing another beating as a result.

My love and loyalty to my mother were repaid with betrayal and lies. When I told her that my stepfather was abusing me, she accused me of making it up. When I plucked up the courage to tell a counselor at our neighborhood Boys & Girls club about the abuse, and child services made the pertinent investigation, my mother told the investigators that I was lying, and the investigation was closed. At every turn I was abused, neglected, and betrayed by the people closest to me.

Finally, at the age of 14, I decided I had had enough, and I left home. For weeks I was homeless, sleeping in abandoned cars and buildings and stealing food to survive. One night, as I was sleeping in a vacant building, I was awakened by several individuals who were armed. I fought off their sexual advances until one put a knife to my throat and threatened to kill me if I did not comply with their sexual demands. At that point, I went into survival mode and did what I had to do to survive the ordeal. Throughout this hellish experience I never got a good look at their faces, and I was never able to identify them.

A few days after I was violently assaulted, I was found sleeping in a garage. The people who found me called the police, and I was placed into foster care. When child services reached my mother, she said I had caused too much trouble with my "false accusations," and she refused to allow me to return home. She left me in foster care for months before finally relenting and letting me back into her home.

My stepfather's abuse started again immediately. I survived for a year in that house before my stepfather almost killed me in a drunken stupor—holding me in the air against a wall by my neck. As he beat me, my mother looked on, doing nothing to protect me. I finally plucked up the courage to give her an ultimatum—it was him, my stepfather, or me, her daughter. She chose the abuser over her own child. At 15, I left home for good.

MY ESCAPE

After I left my mother's house, I did some couch-surfing with friends to have a roof over my head. Despite my lack of home, I still managed to attend school and work.

At 16, I met a handsome, charismatic young man who was in the upper echelon of a prominent gang in the community. After feeling unprotected during my whole childhood, he seemed to be the answer to my prayers—*who would mess with me if I was with him?*— I thought I was in love and soon enough I found myself pregnant at the age of 16. My boyfriend's family took me in, and in April 1985 our son was born. I was a 16-year old, a minor unwed mother on welfare, just another statistic to most.

While I adored—and still adore to this day—my son's grandparents, sadly, shortly after my son's birth, his father revealed to me his violent and controlling nature. He did not allow me to leave the house without him. He had to choose my clothes. He would not allow me to talk to people. In one altercation, he broke my jaw. After escaping my stepfather's abuse, I found myself suffering abuse at the hands of yet another man. Despite his abuse, I did not have the courage to leave him until I learned he had impregnated another girl. Having heard that, I walked out on our five-year relationship and never looked back.

PRIORITIZING MY EDUCATION

After leaving my son's father, I was on my own at 21 years of age with a 4-year-old son. I knew I had to make a better life for him and me. I asked my mother to babysit him, and I got a job at a small law firm in Chicago. Since I never graduated from high school, I went to night classes for my G.E.D., and then started taking college classes at night. I graduated from my local community college with an associate degree and eventually made it to DeVry University and majored in accounting.

At DeVry, I met and fell in love with a fellow student. We dated for a year before he proposed. We got married and we went on to have two wonderful sons fourteen months apart. During my marriage, and despite the fact that I had a job and three little boys, I managed to attend Morton College in Cicero, Illinois, where I earned an associate degree in Criminal Justice. In 2000, I attended MacCormac College in Chicago, where I got an associate degree in Paralegal Studies with honors. I knew I wanted to pursue more education. Unfortunately, my husband chose different paths and eventually got divorced, but we remain good friends with a mutual love and respect for one another and our children and grandchild.

EXPLORING MY ROOTS

At the age of 26, while I was married to my first husband, I applied for a passport. In response, I received a letter from the U.S. State Department saying that the birth certificate I had provided was forged. Shocked, I confronted my mother, who denied it and said she knew nothing about it.

Determined to find my true origin story, I obtained my real birth certificate from Vital Statistics. I was dumbfounded to learn that my mother had altered my certificate to make it look like my sister and I had the same father, when in fact we did not. The name included in my real certificate was that of my mother's first husband, Paul, who fathered her first three children.

I found Paul, who told me that it was possible that he was my biological father; however, a DNA test soon showed that he was not. This was the beginning of my 26-year search for my real father and his family.

FINDING A HOME IN LAW

In 1999, I began dating a family friend and eventually we married in 2001. He had the custody of his three children, we got married and raised our six children together and we bought a home for the huge family. It was full (that is an understatement!) but happy. He supported my desire to further my education, and during our marriage I was able to get a bachelor's degree from the Roosevelt University.

While I was proud to have gotten my paralegal certificate and bachelor's degree, I knew I wanted to aim even higher. In 2003, I started at Cooley Law School in Lansing, Michigan, after local schools waitlisted me. By that time, Cooley was the only school offering weekend classes. For my entire first year of law school, I worked 10 hours per day as a paralegal form Mondays to Thursdays, and then drove to Lansing Michigan every Friday morning to attend classes all weekend. On Sunday afternoons, I drove back to Illinois and started the whole routine over again. I sorely missed my family, but I knew I was building a better life for all of us.

After my first year of law school, I was able to transfer to John Marshall Law School in Chicago, where I attended part-time for five years before I received my Juris Doctor degree.

Unfortunately, my work and law school schedule put an enormous strain on my marriage. After six years of marriage, I was shocked to learn that my husband had a drug problem. Soon enough, I found myself in yet another physically abusive situation, with my husband getting increasingly aggressive and eventually leaving my arms covered in bruises. When my oldest son learned of the abuse, he went after my husband with a bat. So, I packed me and my three children up and filed for divorce the following day.

My own divorce was my source of education, with the courtroom becoming my classroom. It was there that my passion for family law began, as I saw the devastation the litigation process can cause and the need for sound and compassionate practitioners to guide intimidated parties through the harrowing process. By the time my own divorce reached its end, I had completed law school, and I proudly represented myself in court. I am happy to say that my husband eventually sought help for his addiction, and today we are on good terms.

MY CALLING: FAMILY LAW

I was a paralegal for over ten years before I started law

school. While attending law school, I worked with a labor and employment firm, but when the firm downsized, I found myself out of a job right before sitting for my bar exam. As usual, I picked myself right back up and kept moving forward. The first interview I had was with Martoccio&Martoccio, a family law firm. John Martoccio offered me a job as family law associate, and I jumped at it. I have been working in the field of family law ever since.

Today, I am incredibly proud of owning my own law firm, "The Law Offices of Lucy Vazquez-Gonzalez", which I set up in 2017. I handle all types of family law cases, but my true passion lies in my work as guardian *ad litem* ("GAL"), which is an attorney with special training who is appointed by the court to investigate issues regarding parental responsibilities and parenting time and to look out for the best interests of the children involved. I work as a GAL in five different counties in Illinois.

THE FINAL MISSING PIECE: MY FATHER'S FAMILY

For 26 years I have lived with the fact that my father's identity was a mystery, but I never gave up on finding him. Finally, in 2019 I took an Ancestory.com DNA test and was connected with several of my first cousins! Once we found each other, I was thrilled to learn that several of their aunts remembered my mother and sister. Two of my brothers knew about my existence but did not know how to find me. My younger brother had been searching for me but since the information he had was inaccurate, we were unable to meet. Apparently, my parents were living in Lynn, Massachusetts, when my mother abandoned my father, taking me to Chicago and preventing me to have any kind of relationship with him. Tragically, my father died in 2015, before I had the puzzle of my identity solved.

I now know I have three older and two younger siblings. I am grateful to have spent Thanksgiving Day of 2019 with my older sister, older brother, and younger brother! We were not lucky due to the COVID-19 in 2020. Now, I cannot wait to see them all in person sometime soon!

I have been now happily married to my third husband, Luis Gonzalez, for seven years, and I enjoy spending time with my three sons and two grandsons.

MAKING PEACE WITH MY PAIN

Over the years, I have experienced many traumatic flashbacks to terrible events from my past. I understand too well the searing pain and deep anger experienced by survivors. However, do your very best to make peace with your pain and move on with a clear heart and head. That is the only way to truly break the chains that bind you to your trauma and find your life's real purpose. Peace is the greatest gift you can give to yourself.

REFLECTION QUESTIONS

1. Can you understand that your past does not necessarily define your future?

2. Have you found your true calling, your real passion, your home in this world?

3. What can you do to grant yourself peace?

BIOGRAPHY

Lucy Vazquez-Gonzalez is a tough but compassionate family lawyer whose own early trauma defines and guides her work. She is devoted to giving voice to the voiceless through her role as a GAL, advising the court on matters concerning the best interests of children. Being mother to three amazing sons, Lucy overcame her own childhood abuse to get her G.E.D., two associate degrees, a bachelor's degree, and a Juris Doctor degree. She has her own law firm, which she managed to run while raising her children.

Lucy now guides the next generation of lawyers, formally teaching a Family Law/Domestic Violence Clinic at the University of Illinois at the Chicago John Marshall Law School, and at the City Colleges of Chicago and her own alma mater MacCormac College.

Lucy Vazquez-Gonzalez
The Law Offices of Lucy Vazquez-Gonzalez
www.lvglaw.org
attorneylvazquez@yahoo.com
708.813.3273

MY TRIBE, MY COMMUNITY, MY SECRET WEAPON

Carolina M. Veira

"We are the sum of all people we have ever met; you change the tribe, and the tribe changes you."

High school days were rough. I always felt like I did not belong. Most of the other girls at my all-girls high school were skinny, cute, and popular, think *Mean Girls*, but with girls who were actually quite nice; however, in my mind they were different than me in many aspects. We all wore uniforms at school, but during offsite events, my classmates wore stylish clothes, while I wore the hand-me-downs. The majority had brothers and sisters, and I had a son—figuratively. My parents had a baby when I was 10 years old and it forced me to become, in many ways, a mom at age 10. I would take care of my brother while mom was at work, which meant Monday through Sunday. Workaholic anyone?

Instead of high school Saturday events, I spent my weekends studying and babysitting. My dad was a big fan of foreign languages and he made me, and eventually my little brother, learn English, French, German, Portuguese, and any other language we could possibly learn. I would spend Saturday mornings in class and Saturday afternoons working on high school assignments and English presentations, all while feeding and playing with *piojo*, my sweet brother Johnny.

And let me not forget about parties and *quinceañeras*. I remember once I was so looking forward to attending this friend's party, I even convinced my mom to buy me a new dress and she did. She barely said yes to new clothes, at least that is what it seemed to me back then. So, you can imagine this party was the party of the year. The invite read start time 7PM, so of course the party started around 9PM, as all good Hispanic families know, we never start partying early. But my dad, always a rule follower, drove me to the party on time, and I was the first one to arrive. The girl being celebrated was not even ready. There I was sitting in the living room for hours until people started showing up. Right at 10PM when the party was in full motion, my dad picked me up. I remember being so angry at him. He just did not understand what it was to be a teenager with limited opportunities to socialize outside of school. He did not get me. Those were the days.

I always felt like an outsider looking in, I could see the fun my friends were having, but I could not really participate, and in a way, I could not really connect with them. They would talk about the boys they liked, parties and school events they attended on weekends, and I would talk about English competitions, extra-curricular activities and courses I took, books I read, my weekend job at my mom's gas station, and American TV shows I followed. I was always surrounded by people older than me (aunts, uncles, cousins, parents, and grandparents) and conversations were always deeper than teenage conversations. I was the youngest in high school, at home and during English classes; however, I always felt like the oldest teenager on Earth.

MY EARLY TRIBE

I do not want to sound like it was all bad. I was very fortunate to have a big and close family. They always made me feel like my opinion was important. And that made me feel like I could bring my own perspective and it was appreciated. That made me feel confident about my thoughts and feelings. I knew I had to work on other areas, but I never underestimated the power of my ideas and opinions. I owe that to my family, particularly the women. They gave me this sense of security that covered me during those scary years when as teenagers we are trying to understand who we are and how we fit in the world. They are my original tribe.

Things changed after high school graduation, I found a job as a tour guide at *Parque Histórico*, a combination of a small zoo, an *hacienda* and a museum. This place was spectacular. It combined nature, Ecuador's culture, traditions, and our efforts to be sustainable. It was truly visionary. As a tour guide, I could practice all those languages I had learned, and also could make tips. Tips were great! I met wonderful people, co-workers who became great friends. I remember a couple times we would have to hitchhike after work because the park was located about 25 minutes away from the city. I remember us running behind these vehicles many times, jumping in the back of the truck as fast as we could, sitting down and feeling a huge sense of relief. We had made it. I remember the air on my face, the jokes, the stories, and the plans for the weekends. By then I was able to go out to parties and stay out late. My friends would then accompany home. I always felt protected and safe. I knew as long as we were together, everything was going to be okay.

Some of those wonderful humans are still my friends to this day. Despite leaving Ecuador shortly after graduating high school, we managed to be there for each other. They were there for me when I first fell in love and helped me survive my first heartbreak. We celebrated, in person or virtually, birthdays, graduations, weddings, births, divorces, and second marriages together. We travelled together and shared many emails, text messages, Facebook pages and WhatsApp conversations. With them, I discovered the value of having friends who are always there for you, in the good times and the bad times. They are part of my tribe.

NEW HORIZON

Life and my intense desire to learn and grow brought me to the United States. I always knew I would end up living here. I was 12 the first time I watched snow on TV. I remember watching *Home Alone* and being impressed by how the houses and the streets looked all covered in snow. I would tell myself, "This is where I need to be." And it happened, I moved to the US and was blessed with the wonderful opportunity to go to college here. It was a major deal for me. Not everyone could go to college overseas, and it was definitely more challenging to do it in the US. I was proud.

My first day in college in Buffalo, New York was exciting and scary at the same time. Looking back, I know I was one out of the ten Latinos in the whole school. Talk about representation. I always felt like I was representing every Latino in the world. A little extreme I know, but when you are the only one or one of the few, everything seems bigger and more challenging. It feels like you are representing your whole community when you are turning in that paper or presenting in front of your classmates. You must do an impeccable job; you just have to. I was lucky to meet Kat, a beautiful, kind-hearted, energetic Puerto Rican girl who was as proud of her heritage as one could ever be. She was self-made and had experienced challenges in her short life that some of us don't experience in a lifetime. Without knowing, she always made me feel prouder to be Latina. We could be bilingual, enjoy rice and beans, and dance salsa together. Those little pleasures made all the difference in my world. She was part of my tribe.

The school was as international as they could be at that time or for today's standards. The school had an international club and hosted students from countries like Ireland, Vietnam, and Ukraine. I was able to meet and study with amazing humans who also regarded the opportunity to study overseas as the opportunity of a lifetime. Learning from them and their cultures truly made me appreciate my own culture and our common humanity. We all came from different backgrounds and had lived different lives, but somehow managed to find the things that united us. We worked on projects together that allowed us to participate in national tournaments. We travelled, ate, studied, and prepared together. We all appreciated our unique traits and valued our difference in opinions and views. There were great days and not so good ones. We also fought as a family. But in the end, we knew we had to stick together and that made us stronger.

Two of my college professors were instrumental for my professional life. Mr. Eimer, who believed in me more than I believed in myself (most of the time) and was an exceptional coach in the accounting and finance world. He pushed me to always do better without forgetting to be kind to others. He was generous and compassionate. He was like a father to me. He protected us, he valued us, he coached us, he showed that he truly cared for us. It was no coincidence that he worked in healthcare.

And Dr. Kowalewski or Dr. K., our Business Chair and my Leadership professor. She was awesome. I remember her asking me what I wanted to do for the rest of my life, and me saying "I will work in finance, I could be a CFO". Her reply was "Why not a CEO?" Those four words rocked my world. That someone like her could even allow me to dream of becoming a CEO really changed my future. She helped me believe I could. I will be forever thankful to her for being so generous with her words and by doing so, allowing me to dream bigger dreams. They became part of my tribe without even knowing.

HONOR AND PRIDE

After my college years, I was fortunate enough to find other great people who have truly impacted my life. Co-workers who became unconditional friends. Not every co-worker became my best friend, but a few of them became true friends. In my book that is a major win. These friends have carried me in moments of sadness and discouragement, have celebrated with me major life events, and some others have challenged me to see beyond my limitations. Some have been brutally honest when I needed honesty. And some others have been extremely compassionate when I needed advice.

These people, a combination of friends and family, have come together to make a difference in my life. While some of us may not be related through blood, we are profoundly and completely connected through friendship. Those who make up my tribe have become my most incredible supporters. The humans who truly make my life feel complete. Some are no longer part of my daily life, but they are still part of my present, because they helped me become who I am today. My tribe of supporters are those who understand my experiences and push me to do more, be more, and achieve more. In times where I thought I did not belong; they were there to help me understand that this was far from the truth. I will forever be grateful for the contributions they have made to my life.

While they have taught me much over the years, I believe that the greatest gift they have given me is a greater understanding of the meaning behind a family. Through their unlimited support, they have helped me carve out a more profound understanding, a place of appreciation for those we add to our lives. We are the sum of our experiences, our friends, our family. Your tribe is not the group telling us that we are perfect, but the ones who help us stay focused on our path. They help this path become more colorful and joyful. They help us understand our purpose and our why. I love my tribe and its perfect imperfections.

REFLECTION QUESTIONS

1. What are the values and characteristics of your ideal tribe and the people supporting and moving you forward?

2. What is your why and what are your personal values? These are the foundation of your character.

3. Do your personal values and characteristics align with those of your tribe?

BIOGRAPHY

Carolina M. Veira is an authentic leader, financial and business strategist, and Diversity and Inclusion champion, with a passion for the advancement and empowerment of Hispanics, women, and other groups.

Carolina is an award-winning professional and entrepreneur with a successful trajectory in creating community initiatives and strategic partnerships. She believes in the power of building community by working together in financially sustainable and educational initiatives that transform humans and communities.

Carolina earned double Bachelor of Science degrees from D'Youville College in Business and Accounting and a Master's in Business Administration. She is Ecuadorian-American and currently residing in Miami. She enjoys tennis and speaks three languages.

Carolina M. Veira
Email: caro@carolinaveira.com
Website: www.carolinaveira.com
Instagram: @caroveira

Norma Zambrano

"Making a decision is empowering but taking action is transformative."

"You will need to take time to study for the Series 7 exam outside the office," said my manager, convinced I would not go for it. How could I? My daughter was nine years old at that time and my one-year-old boy could not do it without me. I was a mother, a wife, a full-time employee, a leader at my church, and a daughter on a quest to ensure my mom and family could always count on me. For years I would leave the house at 6 a.m. and come back at the end of the day rushing to cook dinner and gather the family to make it to prayer night. Most weekends I would visit Nana and *Abuelo* Hector at their peaceful suburban home with the kids and sometimes I even spent the night there to rest a bit, and went back to Chicago on Sunday to fulfill my responsibilities at the church office since I had been entrusted with all the financial matters, which at times felt like a second full time job.

All my hard work at the bank was paying off and after seven years of being hired, I managed to go up the corporate ladder just enough to occupy the corner office, become a personal banker serving Citigold clients, and experienced in all areas of the bank from teller work, account opening, processing mortgages, establishing retirement plans to sourcing business and investment accounts. Yes, I was doing all that while excelling in service and sales goals. Nothing could stop me! Being a Latina with a heavy accent and having no formal education gave me no other choice.

Why was I even asking my manager to sponsor me for a certification I did not in a million years need for my position? Only Financial Advisers and their assistants were sponsored for this license and allowed time to study during business hours. For me, not getting time during work to study for a 6-hour test that only two out of three people passed should have stopped my ambitious request, but that was not the case! Now, I will tell you why. One day, before moving from my home town of Durango in Mexico to Chicago at the age of 17, I made a decision to go the extra mile, always take the initiative to learn new things no matter how hard or impossible they seemed, and do everything with excellence. So, when I said to my manager: "Yes, I will take time to study outside of work," I had no idea how hard such endeavor would be for me and my family. I devoted three entire months of my life to it! Without fail, every day I would go into the only quiet place in our home, the garage, and study from 6 p.m. to 9 p.m. It was physically and mentally exhausting! I had no social life and missed lots of family gatherings, but all the effort and commitment helped me pass the test on my first try. A huge accomplishment for someone who, as a child, used to think she was not able to achieve anything.

Having a Series 7 license under my belt propelled my career advancement and two years later I was transferred to the private banking division of the company and became part of an elite group of executives that managed a large portfolio of law firms. Eventually, I was appointed vice president. How come? Always remember: Making a decision is empowering, but taking action is transformative.

FUEL YOUR DESIRE TO SUCCEED

"Where is Norma?" my mom would ask everyone, wondering if I was hiding behind the refrigerator, the place I would run to when my dad stopped by the house on his way to *el rancho.* I was so afraid of him! He was a stranger to me. I guess I was four years old the first time he visited us. The second time he stopped by, I was a bit older and I already knew who he was. Although I could see he was the same man that was in the pictures and the stories my mom told us, I did not trust him or want to get close to him at all. When I was old enough to understand my mom was a single mother struggling to make ends meet and working odd jobs to provide our basic needs, I became resentful towards him for having left her with five kids shortly after I was born. I was the youngest and very easy to make fun of. I was a shy and insecure little girl who carried the burden of feelings of worthlessness and bitterness through my teenage years but, at the same time, such feelings fueled a desire to succeed and provide a better life for my mom, the woman that had taught me everything I know and the one I have never wanted to separate from. She was my security blanket.

I was 17 and just starting to feel confident with whom I was becoming. I will never forget the sensation that came to me when I read a letter my mom handed me. It was from the Department of Immigration in Chicago and was certified. "I am not going!" I screamed in anger thinking that my dad's petition to get my visa would disrupt my life as it was. Well, it did! It opened doors for me that allowed me to thrive as a successful executive in the world of investments, it opened doors for me to find love, motherhood, organizations where to serve, and platforms to share knowledge and life experiences. I could have refused to accept it, but I decided to confront the pain from leaving my family and friends in search of the opportunity of a lifetime. Life has shown me not to allow my circumstances to define me, but to fuel my desire to succeed through my circumstances.

WE ALL HAVE A HERO!

When you read the ELISA Foundation memoirs you will better understand why I considered my mom my hero! A piece of me died when she did. She was only 67 but left a legacy that will have a strong impact for centuries to come. As I saw her, there was nothing she could not solve. One of the things I have always admired the most about her is that she never complained about her circumstances and made the best of them.

She was a simple woman without much education, but with the drive and qualities of a world influencer. My mom made use of her abilities to cook and sew to earn her income to support her family and was very entrepreneurial. She was the best dealmaker!

I remember peeping at her at the marketplace getting always the best possible deal without hesitation. My mentor says that "leadership is influence—nothing more, nothing less;" and my mom certainly influenced anyone who got close to her. If you had had the chance to meet her, you would have become a better version of yourself. Her presence in my life was the best coaching experience as to how to deal with anything to leverage the impulse for success. She succeeded in all areas of life and I created the ELISA Foundation in her honor, a 501(c)3, whose name stands for Equipping Leaders to Impact, Serve and Achieve transformation, something she did every day, every minute.

FORGET FAST, FORGIVE FASTER

"Tell him how much you love him," my mom would say as she dictated letters for me to write to my dad when I asked her to help me with the content. I would reluctantly obey to my mom and pray he read the letters and understood how much I longed for having him in my life.

I remember crying myself to sleep many times, especially every birthday he did not show up. He must have visited us three times in my life before I turned fifteen—and always without notice. I never gave up on the hope to have him surprise me for a birthday, but when that was not the case for my fifteenth birthday, one of the most important girl celebrations in Mexico, I was definitely determined not to forget that I was not a good enough reason for him to stay in the marriage and decided to never forgive him. I buried that resentment deep inside well into my twenties and somewhat allowed it to hinder my progress in life—especially in relationships, as I decided not to date anyone and never get married; nevertheless, those feelings once again fueled my desire to succeed. That was the reason why after high school I took an accelerated business administration course and, at the age of sixteen, I was already working at a law firm as secretary, a proof to myself that I could go without a supportive man. The truth is I needed him very much and maybe my mom's constant words of encouragement throughout my childhood to forgive him and love him influenced me to do so.

In September 1993, I made that decision. What a liberating feeling!! I was 26 years old and looking back, my only regret is not having done it earlier. After that, we talked on the phone often and visited his favorite restaurants, *Los Comales* and Atotonilco's in Little Village, Chicago. We started creating nice memories. I still remember the last phone conversation we had. He had moved from Chicago to Missouri a few years before that and would drive back to Chicago at least once a month to get his *queso Chihuahua* and *tortillas El Milagro*. So, when he said on the phone "Mi'ja, I won't be able to drive to Chicago anymore," I said "What? Where will you get your *queso Chihuahua and tortillas del Milagro?* Did you find a place in Missouri?" I could not believe he was giving up on his favorite things in life! We often joked about that and dying young, but this time his voice was different, there was no joking tone so I flew out to see him that weekend only to discover he had been battling with prostate cancer for five years already but decided not to tell us. "Dad, why did you carry this by yourself? You should have told me!" I said. He looked at me and with tears in his eyes he said: "I wanted you to call me because you loved me and not out of pity." This happened two weeks before he would pass away and I will always remember how that weekend helped us both understand our deep love for each other.

God allowed me the opportunity to have a fresh start and experience the liberating feeling of not carrying resentments, anger, or sadness in my heart for the decisions he made, whether right or wrong. That is why I now make forgiveness my supernatural power. I aim to **forget fast and forgive faster.**

REFLECTION QUESTIONS

1. Is there anything you have postponed in your life for not daring to get out of your comfort zone?

2. Who has been a hero in your life and how do you honor that person?

3. Try doing a life-long self-analysis to determine if there is something you need to forget to be able to forgive.

BIOGRAPHY

Norma Zambrano is an international speaker, trainer, and coach focused on helping people grow in all areas of personal development and leadership. She believes that every connection is a world of blessings, she is a passionate philanthropist, creator of the blog *Living a Life of Significance*, a humanitarian entrepreneur, and author of several personal development guides. Her perseverant spirit and acceptance that everything worthwhile does not come easily has been her engine to achieve her goals, which inspire women from all walks of life.

Despite moving to Chicago at 17 without speaking the language and without a formal education, she faced no obstacle big enough to overcome and seize the opportunity to build a rewarding career in one of the largest banking institutions in the world, become VP of the private bank division, and receive the Service Excellence Award—a prestigious recognition only granted to a few employees of the bank worldwide—.

Retiring from Corporate America after more than two decades working in that environment has given her the opportunity to occupy leadership positions in several internationally renowned businesses in both profit and non-profit organizations, the privilege of being the founder of several corporations, and especially the freedom to do what she is passionate about.

One of her greatest achievements has been setting up the ELISA foundation (NFP 501 (c) 3) in honor of her mother to continue her legacy and add value to women who want to be prepared to lead, impact, serve, and achieve transformation in their lives.

Norma is an Independent Executive Director with the John Maxwell team, a facilitator of Change your World roundtable trainings on principles of universal values around the world and a member of the President's Advisory Council of the Maxwell Enterprise.

Norma and her husband reside in Chicago and have two children, a beautiful granddaughter, and an adorable grandson. Her favorite hobbies are traveling, reading, exercising, and spending quality time with her family.

Norma Zambrano
info@normazambrano.com
Instagram: @NPZambrano
www.normazambrano.com

Jacqueline S. Ruíz

**ENTREPRENEUR, AUTHOR, SPEAKER, PILOT,
TODAY'S INSPIRED LATINA FOUNDER**

BIOGRAPHY

Jacqueline S. Ruiz is a visionary social entrepreneur that has created an enterprise of inspiration. Her keen sense of service coupled with the vision to bring good to the world have led her to create two successful award-winning companies, establish two nonprofit organizations, publish 24 books, create over 10 products, and has held dozens of events around the world in just the past decade.

She is often referred to as a "dream catcher" as her strategies have supported thousands of women, authors and young ladies to live a life of significance. Jacqueline's quest to be a servant leader extends to every area of her life. She has shared her inspiration in four continents and aligned with some of the most powerful brands to elevate others. At only 36 years of age, she has achieved what most would not do in an entire lifetime. Being a cancer survivor sparked a sense of urgency to serve and transcend.

Jacqueline believes that magix (yes, a made-up word that means magic x 10) is the interception of profit and impact. She is one of the few Latina sports airplane pilots in the United States and will soon embark on the historic air race that 20 women flyers participated in crossing the United States 91 years ago, including the famous Amelia Earhart.

Jacqueline believes that "taking off is optional, landing on your dreams is mandatory."

For more information, visit www.jackiecamacho.com.